The Rhode Island School of Design
Providence, Rhode Island

Written by Brooke Ackerley
Edited by Alison C. Fleming, Robin Belinsky and Kevin Nash

*Additional contributions by Omid Gohari, Christina Koshzcw,
Chris Mason, Joey Rahimi, and Luke Skurman, and
Kimberly Moore*

ISBN # 1-59658-105-0
ISSN # 1551-997x
© Copyright 2005 College Prowler
All Rights Reserved
Printed in the U.S.A.
www.collegeprowler.com

Special thanks to Babs Carryer, Andy Hannah, Launch-Cyte, Tim O'Brien, Bob Sehlinger, Thomas Emerson, Milton Cofield, Andrew Skurman, Barbara Skurman, Bert Mann, Dave Lehman, Daniel Fayock, Chris Babyak, and The Donald H. Jones Center for Entrepreneurship, Terry Slease, Jerry McGinnis, Bill Ecenberger, Idie McGinty, Kyle Russell, Jacque Zaremba, Larry Winderbaum, Paul Kelly, Roland Allen, Jon Reider, Team Evankovich, Julie Fenstermaker, Lauren Varacalli, Abu Norman, Jason Putorti, Mark Exler, Daniel Steinmeyer, Jared Cohon, Gabriela Oates, Tri Ad Litho, David Koegler, Glen Meakem and The RISD Bounce Back Team.

College Prowler™
5001 Baum Blvd.
Suite 456
Pittsburgh, PA 15213

Phone: (412) 697-1390, 1(800) 290-2682
Fax: (412) 697-1396, 1(800) 772-4972
E-mail: info@collegeprowler.com
Website: www.collegeprowler.com

Welcome to College Prowler™

During the writing of College Prowler's guidebooks, we felt it was critical that our content was unbiased and unaffiliated with any college or university. We think it's important that our readers get honest information and a realistic impression of the student opinions on any campus — that's why if any aspect of a particular school is terrible, we (unlike a campus brochure) intend to publish it. While we do keep an eye out for the occasional extremist — the cheerleader or the cynic — we take pride in letting the students tell it like it is. We strive to create a book that's as representative as possible of each particular campus. Our books cover both the good and the bad, and whether the survey responses point to recurring trends or a variation in opinion, these sentiments are directly and proportionally expressed through our guides.

College Prowler guidebooks are in the hands of students throughout the entire process of their creation. Because you can't make student-written guides without the students, we have students at each campus who help write, randomly survey their peers, edit, layout, and perform accuracy checks on every book that we publish. From the very beginning, student writers gather the most up-to-date stats, facts, and inside information on their colleges. They fill each section with student quotes and summarize the findings in editorial reviews. In addition, each school receives a collection of letter grades (A through F) that reflect student opinion and help to represent contentment, prominence, or satisfaction for each of our 20 specific categories. Just as in grade school, the higher the mark the more content, more prominent, or more satisfied the students are with the particular category.

Once a book is written, additional students serve as editors and check for accuracy even more extensively. Our bounce-back team — a group of randomly selected students who have no involvement with the project — are asked to read over the material in order to help ensure that the book accurately expresses every aspect of the university and its students. This same process is applied to the 200-plus schools College Prowler currently covers. Each book is the result of endless student contributions, hundreds of pages of research and writing, and countless hours of hard work. All of this has led to the creation of a student information network that stretches across the nation to every school that we cover. It's no easy accomplishment, but it's the reason that our guides are such a great resource.

When reading our books and looking at our grades, keep in mind that every college is different and that the students who make up each school are not uniform — as a result, it is important to assess schools on a case-by-case basis. Because it's impossible to summarize an entire school with a single number or description, each book provides a dialogue, not a decision, that's made up of 20 different topics and hundreds of student quotes. In the end, we hope that this guide will serve as a valuable tool in your college selection process. Enjoy!

OMID GOHARI ◯ CHRISTINA KOSHZOW ◯ CHRIS MASON ◯ JOEY RAHIMI ◯ LUKE SKURMAN ◯
The College Prowler™ Team

Table of Contents

Introduction from the Author

Rhode Island School of Design, it's like the Harvard of Art schools. That's the line that almost every student at RISD has had to employ to soothe at least one family member. Once the skeptics get past the initial terror, they swoop in with the flood of questions. Yes, it is a four-year program that gives me a professional degree. Yes, it will help me get a job doing what I love. Yes, artists and designers do need training because raw talent isn't the whole package. Yes, RISD really is considered one of the top art schools in America. No, I can't just go to Harvard, or even Yale, and expect to get the same quality of art education. Now we're past the pleasantries.

Ranging from majors in design to fine art, with concentrations in liberal arts, there is a major and program combination that will suit nearly every serious art student. The thing to keep in mind about RISD is that it will not be an easy ride. To give more perspective, think of it this way: one Freshman Foundations Drawing course lasts eight hours. During these eight hours (with a break for lunch, and whatever other break the individual professor may give) students are expected to stay standing up, with focus on life drawing at the same level as solving math problems. Before they show up to class the following week, they are expected to do fifteen hours of drawing homework for a group critique. One year of this class is required, with students earning three credits per semester for their hard work. Compare this situation with an Ivy League student, who goes to English 101 for a weekly total of ninety minutes, has perhaps five hours of reading and studying to do, and is also provided with three credits per semester. Obviously, the comparison is not quite so simple, but it does illustrate the tremendous time commitment and dedication that it takes to be a RISD student.

The same qualities that make RISD so difficult for students are also what make it a top art school. Professors are dedicated and professional members of their field, who push their students to full capacity, and prepare them for careers that will support them financially and artistically. The resources afforded a RISD student range from top of the line computer labs, to specialized equipment only found in the field, to the RISD Museum. Lastly, every part of the school's environment, from academics to the social scene, pushes students to be who they are as fully as possible, and enable them to make work that is personal and original. That is one of the reasons why RISD alumni are so successful. Aside from the weight of the RISD name, and the tremendous skill range built up over the course of a student's stay, RISD students are original thinkers and problem solvers, and graduate to become leaders of their fields, not following standards, but setting them. When considering an art education, and trying to decipher between another art school and The Rhode Island School of Design, the truly important question to ask is not "is art the best I can do?" but "how good can I really be"?

Brooke Ackerley, Author
Rhode Island School of Design

By the Numbers

General Information

Rhode Island School of Design
2 College St
Providence, RI 02903

Control:
Private

Academic Calendar:
4-1-4

Religious Affiliation:
None

Founded:
1877

Website:
www.risd.edu

Main Phone:
(401) 454-6100

Admissions Phone:
(401) 454-6300

Student Body

Full-Time Undergraduates:
1,920

Part-Time Undergraduates:
0

Female: Male Ratio:
65:35

Full-Time Male Undergraduates:
681

Full-Time Female Undergraduates:
1,239

Admissions

Overall Acceptance Rate:
35%

**Early Decision
Acceptance Rate:**
N/A

Regular Acceptance Rate:
33%

Total Applicants:
2,420

Total Acceptances:
835

Freshman Enrollment:
391

**Yield (% of admitted
students who actually enroll):**
47%

**Applicants Placed on Waiting
List:**
N/A

**Transfer applications
received:**
667

**Transfer applicants offered
admission:**
155

Transfer applicants enrolled:
119

**Transfer Applicant
Acceptance Rate**
23%

Early Decision Available?
No

Early Action Available?
Yes

Early Action Deadline:
December 15

Early Action Notification:
Last week of January

Regular Decision Deadline:
February 15

**Regular Decision
Notification:**
April 1

Must-Reply-By Date:
May 1

**Common Application
Accepted?**
No

Supplemental Forms?
A portfolio of work is
mandatory, along with three
original drawings that satisfy
certain specifications.

Admissions Phone:
(401) 454-6300

Admissions E-mail:
admissions@risd.edu

Admissions Website:
http://www.risd.edu

➜

SAT I or ACT Required?
Either

**First-Year Students
Submitting SAT Scores:**
94%

**SAT I Range
(25th – 75th Percentile):**
1090-1310

**SAT I Verbal Range
(25th – 75th Percentile):**
540-650

**SAT I Math Range
(25th – 75th Percentile):**
550-660

Retention Rate:
93%

**Top 10% of
High School Class:**
34%

Financial Information

Full-Time Tuition:
$27,975

Application Fee:
$50

Room and Board:
$7,720

Books and Supplies for class:
$1,800

Other Fees:
$500

**Average Need-Based
Financial Aid Package:**
$11,450

**Students Who
Applied For Financial Aid:**
59%

**Students Who Received
Aid:**
67%

Financial Aid Forms Deadline:
February 15

Financial Aid Phone:
(401) 454-6661

Financial Aid E-mail:
priefler@risd.edu

Financial Aid Website:
http://www.risd.edu/financial_
aid.cfm

Academics

The Lowdown On...
Academics

Degrees Awarded:
BFA, MFA

Most Popular Majors:
55% Fine and Studio Art
13% Commercial Art
12% Architecture
11% Industrial Design

Full-Time Faculty:
176

Faculty with Terminal Degree:
79%

Student-to-Faculty Ratio:
11:1

Average Course Load:
12-15 credits (3 studios,1 or 2 liberal arts)

Undergraduate Schools
School of Design
School of Fine Art

Special Degree Options
5-Year BARCH, BIA, BID, BGD, 3-Year MID, MIA, MARCH, MA, MAT, MLA

AP Test Score Requirements
Possible credit for scores of 4 or 5

IB Test Score Requirements
Possible credit for scores of 5, 6, and 7

Graduation Rate:
Four-years : 87%
Five-years: 90%
Six-years: 90%

Best Places to Study
Library, Local Coffeehouses

Sample Academic Clubs
Mixed Media, the school newspaper
Blackletter literary magazine

Did You Know?

RISD students may register for **Brown University** classes.

- Among other study abroad programs, RISD has a **European Honors Program** that allows students to study in Rome for a year.

• RISD has **a mini-semester in January, called Wintersession**, during which students are offered experimental courses, travel courses, and internship opportunities.

Academics

"Most of the teachers have been spectacular. In four years I've had three bad teachers, but my peers have always made the class better. My classes also have mostly been very rewarding."

Q "My profs have been so **helpful and professional.** They really care about us as students."

Q "They are **amazing, intriguing, and great.** I learn so much from them. Everyone is helpful and open to independent study. I find my classes very interesting and challenging."

Q "Some studio classes are interesting, but **most liberal-arts classes are jokes.**"

Q "Both teachers and **classes vary drastically.** They're either really wonderful and awe-inspiring, or they're terrible!"

Q "It's hard to generalize about such a diverse faculty and course offerings. I will say that I have had at least one really amazing teacher every semester as well as at least one interesting class. Overall I think that the classes get more genuinely interesting as you go along and can specialize more and have more **freedom in choosing your own classes.**"

Q "Teachers here are very passionate about what they are teaching. I find my classes interesting because of that. **Calling them by their first names** makes them more like friends."

Q "I have encountered various teachers, both good and bad. For the most part it really impresses me that there are teachers who are willing to **sacrifice their personal time to help their students** I have professors who come in to give me extra help during Sunday mornings; I also had another teacher who came in late during the night and stayed with me until Midnight to help me with my work. On that note I feel like RISD teachers are some of the most dedicated and caring teachers I have ever met in my life."

Q "Almost the only teachers that I have had that I would consider bad were in Foundation Year. Everything is less specialized and it doesn't seem they're quite as into the class. But then again, it really **depends on what teachers you happened to get."**

Q "There are **too many RISD alumni as teachers**. However, if you get into the right class, it's very interesting."

Q "Most of the teachers I have had here have a lot of expectations of their students. **They are dedicated and driven** and will go out of their way to help students, giving them just as much back as the students put in. My classes are very interesting."

Q "Almost all of my major teachers have been so invested that I'm sure **they don't get paid enough for what they do.** We have all the contact info for them and there's been many times where I was having a problem in studio at ten at night and I could call my professor and she talked me through it, or came in to help."

The College Prowler Take On...
Academics

Academics at RISD are based on a number of variables, two of which being what major you choose, and whether you decide to "concentrate" in a liberal-arts field. The differences in majors have to do with departmental budgets and resources, individual faculty members, and overall departmental philosophy. Each major has a different number of required major credits, with some allowing students to take more classes outside their major, and others almost taking up a student's entire studio course load. Regardless of major, studio classes are almost always challenging and enriching, and demand all of a student's resources to complete them successfully.

The faculty is the driving force behind RISD's strenuous and exiting classes. It is safe to say that while there may be the odd professor that does not meet what the high-standard students expect from their faculty, professors at RISD are professional, knowledgeable, and dedicated to their students and their field. When it comes to Liberal Arts, students may "concentrate", which is similar to having a minor, in English, Art History, or HPSS (History, Philosophy, Social Science). These concentrators, who put more effort into their Liberal Arts experience, tend to come away more satisfied with their classes because their academic study interacts more with their studio study, bringing it to a higher level. While it's true that some liberal-arts courses may not be as rigorous, nearly all seminar courses, among others, are just as challenging as an equivalent class at almost any liberal-arts university.

The College Prowler™ Grade on
Academics: B

A high Academics grade generally indicates that professors are knowledgeable, accessible, and genuinely interested in their students' welfare. Other determining factors include class size, how well professors communicate, and whether or not classes are engaging.

Local Atmosphere

The Lowdown On...
Local Atmosphere

Region:
Northeast

City, State:
Providence, Rhode Island

Setting:
Urban

Distance from NY:
Approx. 180 miles

Distance from Boston:
Approx. 50 miles

Points of Interest:
The First Baptist Church of America
Narragansett Bay
Local Galleries
Russian Submarine Museum
Waterplace Park/River Walk
Fleet Skating Center
RISD Museum
The Culinary History Museum
Slater Mill Museum
The John Brown House
Providence Repertory Company

Closest Movie Theatres:

National Amusements
Providence Place 16
Providence Place Mall
5 Providence Place
(401) 270-4646

Feinstein IMAX Theater
Providence Place Mall
5 Providence Place
(401) 453-IMAX

Avon Cinema
260 Thayer St.
(401) 421-AVON

Cable Car Cinema and Cafe
204 South Main St.
(401) 272-3970

Major Sports Teams:
Boston Red Sox
New England Patriots

Closest Shopping Malls:

The Arcade
65 Weybosset Street
Providence RI 02903
(401) 598-1049

Providence Place Mall
5 Providence Place
Providence, RI 02903
(401) 270-4370

Wickenden Street and Thayer Street also have a variety of good shops.

City Websites
http://www.providenceri.com
http://www.goprovidence.com

Did You Know?

Fun Facts about Providence:

- **Most streets aren't labeled**, which makes for crazy adventures.
- Providence began as **a haven for Puritans**.
- Due to a clerical error in the late 1800s, for a time, "Providence" was **the official Rhode Island state bird**.
- Former Mayor, **"Buddy" Cianci**, has received the most votes for public office while serving probation or jail time since Eugene Debbs in WWI.
- Providence was **the birthplace of pulp horror novelist H.P. Lovecraft**, and served as a temporary home to Edgar Allen Poe.
- CNN's Money Magazine labeled Providence, **"The Best Place to Live in the East"** for two years in a row, 2000 and 2001.
- Rhode Island has **more than 400 miles of ocean shoreline** and RISD owns a farm with 33 acres of lawn and beach front on Narragansett Bay.
- Providence is home to **the oldest mall in America**, the Arcade, built in 1829.

Famous People from Providence:

H.P. Lovecraft, Spalding Gray, Jeanine Garaffalo, George Michael Cohan, Horace Mann, Julia Ward Howe, Samuel Slater, Harry Anderson, Roger Williams, Nicholas Brown.

Local Slang

Wicked = Very

Soggie = A greasy hotdog

Cab'nit = A milkshake

Downcity = Downtown Providence

Dels = A slushy drink

Take a Hat = Have a heart attack

Quahogs = Clams

Students Speak Out On...
Local Atmosphere

"Providence is nice for being at college. There's some stuff to do, but not too much to get distracted. I thought I'd have more time to go to NY and Boston, though."

Q "The atmosphere is okay, I guess. **I don't really think there is one distinct atmosphere for the entire city**. There are bad areas; ones to stay away from, but nothing close enough for a RISD student to really wander into."

Q **"Providence is a paper city**—it's really weird, go to 80's Night till it's boring, and go to shows in whatever warehouses are left."

Q "The atmosphere is a **college little city**. Downtown and certain areas can be scary late at night, if alone. But I'm comfortable."

Q "**Providence is a small, big city**—not as big as NY, bigger than Worcester."

Q "Honestly, I don't think there's much to do in Providence in terms of entertainment, since I grew up in a big city. You really need to **get out there to discover things you want to do.** However, I like going to Federal Hill to have a nice dinner with my friends on special occasions (Pastiche is a fantastic bakery place). I also enjoy watching theatrical plays at Trinity Repertory and even the Perishable Theatre downtown. Sometimes it's also nice when I get to go to Asian or Chinese restaurants like King's Garden on Park Avenue, or Lucky Garden on Smith Street."

Q "**Providence is a weird, big college/colonial town.** Stay away from the downtown transit area. Visit Wickenden St., Thayer St., Brown University, and Downtown. Visit the old buildings and the capitol building."

Q "Obviously **visit the RISD Museum** and other galleries scattered throughout. Those things are underused."

Q "The **East Side and College Hill are rather student friendly.** It's not a large city, it's pretty small actually, but it still has the same kinds of benefits that a larger city has. I wouldn't venture out into the South End of Providence alone at night."

Q "**The atmosphere's New England-y**. Visit the Russian Sub."

The College Prowler Take On...
Local Atmosphere

Providence, Rhode Island is absolutely New England. It is the largest city in New England outside Boston, and behaves accordingly. While culturally Boston is a big leap from Providence, there are things about the city that make it wonderful. One such thing is the once a month celebration of Waterfire. This is a celebration of the art of Providence that includes lighted piles of wood all along the canal and ambient music that fills the streets until midnight. Other wonderful things are Providence's museums and galleries, the shops, and the food. Federal Hill is the mostly Italian section of Providence that hosts some of the best restaurants in the area. While there is a definite city feel, Providence is not devoid of green space, and there are several parks within walking distance that give really pleasant views of the city and its waterfront.

The main activity in Providence is built on the colleges of RISD, Brown, and Johnson and Wales, and so the town caters much of its business and attitude toward college students. The surrounding college neighborhoods are fairly quiet and pleasantly residential, and Providence is full of historic buildings, that give it the small-town feel that you can't often get while being exposed to the resources of a city. It's the benefit of being in a college town, without the complete bubble. Providence's size keeps it very accessible and it doesn't take long to know your way around. If you're looking for a taste of the bigger city, New York is fairly close by, and a Commuter Rail train will take you to Boston during the week for six dollars. In many ways, Providence has the ability to satisfy and frustrate everyone. It does not have the same excitement and culture of New York, and it doesn't have the natural beauty of the American West, but rather sits in a perfect middle ground, and will give you a little taste of both.

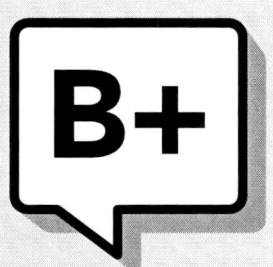

The College Prowler™ Grade on
Local
Atmosphere: B+

A high Local Atmosphere grade indicates that the area surrounding campus is safe and scenic. Other factors include nearby attractions, proximity to other schools, and the town's attitude toward students

Safety & Security

The Lowdown On...
Safety & Security

Public Safety:

Public Safety

30 Waterman St.

Open 24 hours/7 days a week

Number of RISD Police:

42

Phone:

(401) 454-6376

(401) 454-6666 - emergencies

Safety Services:

Campus foot patrol

Bicycle and marked cruisers

Emergency Call Boxes

SAFEWALK

SAFERIDE

Key card access to certain buildings

Strict building hours

Self Defense Classes

Health Services:

Homer Hall

55 Angell St.

(401) 454-6625

There is an on-duty nurse and physician on call, some testing can be done by the physician during certain hours of the day. They provide health promotion, protection, education, disease prevention clinical care, and basic psychological and counseling services.

Health Center Office Hours

Monday – Friday 8:30 a.m. – 8:30 p.m., Saturday 9 a.m. – 5 p.m., Sundays and Holidays Noon – 7:30 p.m.

Did You Know?

 **Most crimes actually happen on Brown campus** or the surrounding area, but not actually on RISD campus.

Students Speak Out On...
Safety & Security

"I feel safe in the buildings and in the center of campus. It's a city, though, and looks sweeter than it is."

Q "**It's very safe and** security is great."

Q "We're in a city. We try to stay safe, and our **Public Safety officers do the best they can**. The only thing that has been not so effective is our SAFERIDE."

Q "Public Safety are constantly **power tripping and harassing kids,** you will without a doubt have a run-in with a Public Safety officer."

Q "It's safe. Providence is a city; **muggings are a reality,** but happen infrequently."

Q "On campus it's pretty good. **The shuttle system has improved greatly,** meaning you never have to be walking home alone at night. For a city of its size, Providence is not a very dangerous place and the RISD area is the poshest section of Providence. You shouldn't be out alone at 2 a.m. or leave expensive electronics around, but I feel safe enough."

Q "It seems like **Brown kids get mugged more than we do**, but supposedly it happens to us too."

Q "**I think it's pretty safe and secure on campus**. I never like walking alone on Thayer St. in the middle of the night, it scares me. Also I wouldn't walk alone near the East Side of Providence like where Brook and Arnold St. intersect. That park over there is very sketchy at night. I think SAFERIDE is doing a fantastic job sending students from on-campus areas to off-campus areas."

Q "I think campus feels pretty safe, most of the time, but I get a little skittish walking around at three in the morning. I wouldn't walk around on parts other than Thayer St. and Wickenden St. by myself after dark. **Definitely travel in groups after dark when off campus.**"

Q "Security is pretty good. **They're pretty strict about getting doors locked** and who has access to rooms."

The College Prowler Take On...
Safety & Security

Even though Providence is a city, most students feel safe while they're on campus and the close surrounding areas. The blue emergency phones, Public Safety Officers' patrol, strict building access, and SAFERIDE system keep the feeling of on-campus safety high. RISD's SAFERIDE van system is in a partnership with Brown SAFERIDE. It provides shuttle service to RISD students from the hours of five in the evening to three in the morning, and will take students from a residence to campus, or campus to residence. Students who live on campus may catch the shuttle during its regular stops along a fixed route. Students living off campus may call for a specific pickup and will be reached within fifteen minutes. While it is still in the process of being improved and refined, SAFERIDE is not completely satisfactory. There is a route that the shuttle adheres to that circumnavigates the area in which most students live. However, there are students who live outside of this area who have been left out of the SAFERIDE loop.

While most students feel safe on campus, they also have had some conflict with the officers who carry out this objective. It is to be expected that such figures of authority may rub students the wrong way from time to time. Often these run-ins have to do with officers who are trying to close studio buildings while students are trying to stay and finish their work. However, representatives of Public Safety are often in communication with student groups in order to find out how they may better protect the student community. A new policy in which individual Public Safety officers are assigned to each student house is an effort not to police students, but to increase communication and improve relations.

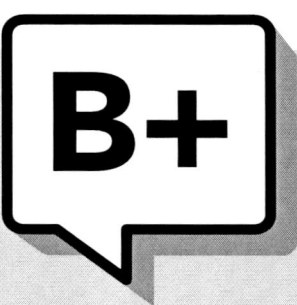

The College Prowler™ Grade on

Safety &
Security: B+

A high grade in Safety & Security means that students generally feel safe, campus police are visible, blue-light phones and escort services are readily available, and safety precautions are not overly necessary.

Computers

The Lowdown On...
Computers

High-Speed Network?
Yes

Numbers of Computers:
Over 400

Wireless Network?
Yes

Operating Systems:
PC, Mac, and UNIX

Number of Labs:
Approx. 14

Discounted Software

The only discounted software available comes in the package required of the laptop program buyers

Free Software

Anti-virus program- If you bring your computer to CNS, they will install an anti-virus program, but they won't give you a hard copy.

24-Hour Labs

None

Charge to Print?

8.5"x 11" - 10 cents black and white, $1.00 color

These charges are made to pre-paid print cards, but they do not apply the same to Graphic Design students who are printing a mile a minute.

Did You Know?

Many majors have their own "CAD" programs. Everyone knows that **Architects use AutoCAD**, but did you know that Textiles, Furniture, ID, Glass, and even Apparel have their own CAD programs?

Students Speak Out On...
Computers

"The computer labs never seem overcrowded. Bringing a personal computer and basic printer is ideal because it will save travel time and hassle."

Q "Bring your own computer if you can—**the network is constantly down** for periods of time."

Q "The computer network is ok. It depends on what you need it for. Most of the computer-heavy departments have their own labs or require students to purchase their own laptops, so crowding in communal labs isn't a problem. Sometimes **the lab hours aren't the best** or monitors fail to show up, but I wouldn't go so far as to recommend bringing a computer in order to avoid the labs."

Q "Bring your own computer and a printer to avoid hassle. If you're in a certain major, **they'll make you buy a laptop.**"

Q "The network is **good for e-mail, but difficult for online recourses** (online storage is not always available). We need a Mac-based network so we wouldn't suffer from IBM viruses. The labs are usually busy. I use RISD-ROMEABOUT often."

Q **"CNS is terrible!** The only help you can get is from other students. Don't buy a computer if you're going into a major with the laptop program."

Q "From the experience of working in the AMC lab in the 2nd floor of the Design Center for almost an entire year, I don't think that Computer Network Services is very good with maintaining the G5 Macs they have. A lot of them have network issues and **won't let you log in properly, or won't print properly.** Now I don't even use the Mac labs since I have my own laptop and printer. Personally, I think it's ridiculous that we have to pay to print black and white, and even more ridiculous to pay a dollar for each A4-sized printed color copy."

Q "I can't concentrate on writing papers and doing major stuff in a lab, so **I brought a computer, and it's been essential**. I didn't go into the laptop program, though. A lot of kids that end up in those majors sell the computers they had cheap, so you could always come and buy one off someone else."

Q "The **computers at school are really nice and really fast.** There are a number of labs across campus so they are rarely really crowded, maybe during finals week. If you have one, bring it, that's nice too. The network often has issues and can be annoying."

Q "Really **what we need computers for is all the design stuff.** It doesn't really help to bring a computer for that because you'll be using programs that the school has to license only to it's controlled labs. However, if you're into academics and plan on 'concentrating' and writing a lot of papers it may be helpful."

The College Prowler Take On...
Computers

It may sound surprising for an art school, but computers are actually a big part of most major curriculums at RISD. Many majors use CAD (Computer Assisted Design) programs in their curricula in order to prepare students for competitive job markets, as well as the different ways that they may approach their art on a personal level. If you already have your own computer and printer, they are extremely handy to have at school. However, there is a chance that you will enter a major that will require you to purchase a very expensive laptop package through the school, so it is a really bad idea to buy a computer before you come. Also, even if your major does not participate in the laptop program you may have to learn CAD programs for which there will be plenty of computers available, because you would not be able to obtain the appropriate software for a personal computer.

Aside from the more major-specific labs that have certain CAD programs on them, there are general labs that students may use to type and print papers and use the internet. These labs are equipped with several computer stations, usually two flatbed scanners and a negative scanner, and two LaserJet printers, one color, one black and white. Students who sign in and are recognized by the network may print from any computer station and get their work within a matter of seconds. Also, almost all the labs on campus are networked. This means that if the printer is down in one lab, a student may put work on the network space and then go and print it in another lab. RISD also has a wireless network, but in order to print work, a student must send a project to the printer from a physical computer station in one of the labs. The network is fairly reliable, although it does go down from time to time. The computers in the labs are replaced every few years and you will always have the newest versions of programs with fairly new computers. The lab resources are sufficient and labs are rarely overcrowded.

The College Prowler™ Grade on

Computers: B

A high grade in Computers designates that computer labs are available, the computer network is easily accessible, and the campus' computing technology is up-to-date.

Facilities

The Lowdown On...
Facilities

Campus Size:
49 acres

Student Center:
Coming soon, until then, whatever space can be found is used.

Athletic Center:
Catanzaro Fitness Center (RISD students may use all Brown athletic facilities)

Libraries:
RISD Library
Nature Lab
Picture Collection
(RISD students may enter and sometimes check outmaterial from all Brown libraries)
(RISD students may also use the Providence Athenaeum)

Popular Places to Chill:
The Beach, in front of Mem Hall, Dorm Lounges, the Quad, the Met (main dining facility), in studio.

What Is There to Do On Campus?

- RISD Film Society film showings held in the Auditorium and Tap Room

- Student and Professional Poetry Readings in Carr Haus

- Guest Lecturers in the Auditorium, in individual departments

- Student Gallery Showings at: The Red Eye Gallery, The Red Door Gallery, Carr Haus, Woods Gerry Gallery, First Floor Design Center Gallery, Sol Koffler Graduate Student Gallery

- Play ping pong and pool in the Homer Lounge

- Admission to the Museum is free for RISD students.

- The Edna Lawrence Nature Lab and the RISD Picture Collection are amazing resources.

- The Nature Lab, in the Freshmen Foundation building is a three-dimensional library of specimens and live creatures. Many things may not be checked out, but students bring their work with them, and draw, paint, or sculpt in the Lab while looking at taxidermied animals and fetuses in jars.

- The Picture Collection in the RISD Library is a clipping file of thousands of pictures arranged by category available for check out.

Movie Theatre on Campus?

No, but there are sometimes movie showings in the Auditorium and Tap Room

Bar on Campus?

No

Bowling on Campus?

No

Did You Know?

Many of the RISD buildings are **haunted**!
(See Page 113 *Urban Legends*)

Coffeehouse on Campus?

Carr Haus, on the corner of Waterman St. and Benefit St. is a coffeehouse and café open only on the weekdays.

Watermark Café, 2nd floor of the RISD Store in the Design Center at 30 North Main St. open on the weekdays.

Favorite Things to Do

Walk around

See independent films

Shop

Go to coffeehouses

Hang out in a laid back bar.

Students Speak Out On...
Facilities

"We'll probably always want more in our studios. But I think compared to other schools, we have amazing recourses. My department has equipment that only exists at a couple schools in the country."

"**Studios are cool,** the new computers are cool, the old ones are okay. We need all Mac screens, but other than that, all of the peripheral supplies are awesome."

"The computers are fine, the gym is okay. Studios are fine, but be careful! **They will say you can use any facilities, (furniture, woodshops) and it's a lie!** You need to know someone in that department."

"**Some departments are a lot nicer and newer than others** as far as facilities. The computers are all pretty new/fast, the gym is mediocre, but we can use the very nice Brown gym instead."

"I honestly wish RISD had its own swimming pool! I wouldn't mind going swimming. **I don't think there are enough athletic facilities on campus**, but at the same time it's nice that we get to share facilities with Brown. Although RISD has a lot of computer labs located around campus, I honestly don't think they're again, well-maintained. I think RISD's studio facilities are really great, although I've encountered serious space issues in terms of the Textile department during my sophomore and junior years. It's okay during our senior year since we actually have our personal studio space."

Q "Our athletic facilities are good, but I've heard Brown is nicer. Our color printers often fail, the studios are good, but **people do not clean up after themselves.** The dorm studios are messy, but it's nice that they're there."

Q "Our ID facilities are okay. **The shops (wood, metal) are nice.**"

Q "It depends on your major—my studios are unbelievable. **They put a million resources at your fingertips.** And the atmosphere is great for working. I haven't really heard people that upset about communal studios; it's more a fight for personal studio space. Some majors get more than others, and not until a certain year, if at all."

Q **"Printmaking studios are crammed."**

Q "The facilities are nice but since **they are old buildings they are built in an odd way.** The architecture's funny."

Q "Athletics and computers are good. **The Dining is pretty good**. The studios depend on the department. I don't have my own (photo lab), so that's too bad."

Q "I've been really impressed with my department. My class doubled the size of the previous class, and **they've found a way to accommodate us at every turn**. It's been tight in some cases, the CAD lab is the worst, but we've managed."

The College Prowler Take On...
Facilities

When it comes to studio space, (which is the facility that students care about most) it's on a department by department basis. On the whole, people's needs are met one way or another. When it comes to athletic facilities, Brown makes up for what RISD lacks. When it comes to computers, the communal labs satisfy anyone who doesn't need extremely specific programs, and then certain majors have their own labs to fulfill those needs (an example of this would be the need for CAD programs in different departments). When it comes to studio space, most everyone has what they need to function.

The equipment that RISD students are privileged to have access to during their college experience is impressive. For example, there are approximately six wood shops on campus that grant access to different groups of students, and the Textiles department has one of two college-owned Jacquard looms in the country. Aside from these kinds of departmental resources, RISD's greatest resource is the Museum. Admission is free to all RISD students, and sometimes events are planned specifically for them, as well as the yearly showing of graduate-student work, and the winners of the contest "Sightings". The best part about the museum is that if you make an appointment far enough in advance, you can meet with a curator or assistant, and they will pull almost any part of the collection for you to see in person. Considering that at the current time, only four percent of the collection is on display, RISD students are given access to a tremendous resource that is not afforded anyone else.

B-

The College Prowler™ Grade on

Facilities: B-

A high Facilities grade indicates that the campus is aesthetically pleasing and well-maintained; facilities are state-of-the-art, and libraries are exceptional. Other determining factors include the quality of both athletic and student centers and an abundance of things to do on campus.

Campus Dining

The Lowdown On...
Campus Dining

Freshman Meal Plan Requirement?

Yes

Meal Plan Average Cost:

Freshman plan is $3,000/year

Places to Grab a Bite with Your Meal Plan

The Break

Location: Lobby of the Providence Washington building

Food: Sandwiches to go, snacks, coffee

Favorite Dish: Grilled Chicken Caesar Wrap

Hours: Monday-Friday 7:30 a.m. – 3:00 p.m.

Carr Haus

Location: Corner of Waterman St. and Benefit St.

Food: Café Sandwiches, Pastries, Coffees

Favorite Dish: Spinach Calzone

Hours: Monday and Friday 8 a.m.-8 p.m., Tuesday-Thursday 8 a.m.-2 a.m.

The Met

(Main Dining Facility)

Location: Freshman Quad

Food: Salad, Sandwich, Vegan Bar, Bakery, Pizza, Full Entrees, Full Breakfast, Lunch, Dinner

Favorite Dish: Pad Thai, Battered Cod

Hours: Monday-Thursday 7 a.m.-2 a.m., Saturday 7 a.m.-8 p.m., Sunday 12 p.m.-2 a.m

The Pit

Location: First Floor of Memorial Hall

Food: Burgers, Grilled Sandwiches, Breakfast Sandwiches, Snacks

Favorite Dish: Shaved Steak Sandwich

Hours: Monday-Thursday 10 a.m.-8 p.m., Fri 10 a.m.-3 p.m.

Watermark Café

Location: Above RISD store in the Design Center

Food: Fancy Vegetarian/Vegan Fare

Favorite Dish: Caesar Salad

Hours:Monday-Thursday 9 a.m.-6 p.m., Friday 9 a.m.-3 p.m.

Student Favorites:
Carr Haus, Watermark Cafe

Off-Campus Places to Use Your Meal Plan:
None

24-Hour On-Campus Eating?
No

Did You Know?

- You can **order birthday cakes** through The Met.
- **Carr Haus** is student-run and student-employed.
- You can **bring the Met a recipe from home** (within reason) and they will serve it on the menu.

Students Speak Out On...
Campus Dining

"The breakfast menu at the cafeteria never changes and the eggs are not real, but it's very sanitary."

Q "The food on campus is improving. **The Met needs to offer more vegan options**, and more cashiers to avoid long lines."

Q "For campus food, it's quite good. **You get sick of it by the second half of your freshman year,** but it's still pretty good. There are always vegetarian and vegan options and lots of 'do-it-yourself' salad/sandwich stuff. Carr Haus has good baked goods but vile coffee. The new RISD Watermark Café is great quality, but pricey."

Q "**The Met is better than other schools,** but that's not saying much."

Q "**For Vegans it's pretty good**, actually, very good. The Watermark Café is good."

Q "The food on campus is actually not so bad compared to the campus food at Brown. I personally like hanging out a lot in Carr Haus and the Pit, **they make good food and it's a great environment** to stay in especially because they're more personal. I like Carr Haus a lot since that's where I go to meet people and friends who are out of my major. The Met food is actually improving. I've worked with the Dining Services Committee and I think they're trying hard to improve their food by all means."

Q "On campus, the food's good but **the service is not so good."**

Q "The food at **Carr Haus is the best, but that's where the longest line is,** usually. With the Met, you really have to be on the meal plan to afford the prices. The Pit is good grilled stuff, but it gets real old real fast, and it's sometimes too greasy. I haven't eaten much at the Break because it's way out of the way. And Watermark Café is great, but really, really expensive for school food."

Q "The food is actually really, really good. Compared to other schools, it's excellent. I've had friends come over excited to eat at the Met with me. Carr Haus (campus coffee house) is excellent. **The dining halls don't have much atmosphere, but the food is good."**

Q "The food is **good in comparison to the other schools** I've visited."

The College Prowler Take On...
Campus Dining

Students will always, always complain about school food. Anyone eating the same things every day for every meal is bound to get sick of them. However, if you ask freshmen in the first month of school, they'll tell you how great the food is. It's diverse, there are always vegetarian options and vegan options, it's accessible, it's tasty, and it's healthy. Many of the cooks are Johnson and Wales graduates or interns, so there is a certain culinary flair to most dishes. Also, to give some perspective, the Met, which is the main dining center, caters most school functions, so the administration must think the food is good. Most of the food in the Met is sold by weight, so you get what you pay for, and you're not charged for a "meal" if you just want to come in and get an apple and a drink. Except for Carr Haus, the food is fairly expensive for kids who are not on the meal plan, but if you are on the meal plan, it will give you enough points to eat comfortably. The Met also takes special care in trying to accommodate the foods that students may miss from home. There is always a suggestion box so that students may make requests or submit recipes.

There are four meal-plan options. Freshmen are required to purchase the largest plan, which is good and bad. No one wants to run out of money for food, however, most kids can't eat enough to use their points, and the school only gives back a small percentage of what's left if it's over $100. Many kids who have extra money end up paying for their few friends who have run out, and the Mug Sale in Carr Haus takes care of the rest. There are plenty of creative ways to use points. Sometimes students bring in baked goods for the last day of classes as a celebration, and some give food to shelters.

The College Prowler™ Grade on

Campus Dining: B-

Our grade on Campus Dining addresses the quality of both school-owned dining halls and independent on-campus restaurants as well as the price, availability, and variety of food.

Off-Campus Dining

The Lowdown On...
Off-Campus Dining

Restaurant Prowler:
Popular Places to Eat!

Antonio's by the Slice
Food: Pizza
Address: 258 Thayer St.
Phone: (401) 455-3600
Cool Features: Good pizza, extra cheap.
Price: $2 per slice
Hours: Sunday-Monday 11 a.m. – 1 a.m.

Asian Paradise
Food: Chinese, Vietnamese, Cambodian, Korean
Address: 165 S Angell St.
Phone: (401) 454-0222
Cool Features: Unusual range of Asian food
Price: $8 and under per person
Hours: Sunday- Thursday 11:30 a.m.-10 p.m., Friday-Saturday 11:30 a.m.-11 p.m.

Bombay Club

Food: Indian

Address: 145 Dean St.

Phone: (401) 273-6363

Cool Features: The best Indian in Providence

Price: $15 and under per person

Hours: Monday-Saturday 11:30 a.m. – 3 p.m., and 5:00 p.m. – 11:00 p.m., Sunday 12:30 p.m. – 3:00 p.m., and 5:00 p.m. – 10:30 p.m.

The Creperie

Food: Crepes of all kinds

Address: 82 Fones Alley

Phone: (401) 751-5536

Cool Features: A Crepe for a meal

Price: $6 and under per person

Hours: Monday-Thursday 10 a.m.–12 p.m., Friday 10 a.m.-2 a.m., Saturday 9 a.m.– 2 a.m., Sunday 9 a.m. – 12 p.m.

Cuban Revolution Cafe

Food: Cuban

Address: 149 Washington St

Phone: (401) 331-8829

Cool Features: Lots of cool art on the walls, live music, no cover.

Price: $10 and under per person

Hours: Monday – Saturday 11 a.m. - Midnight

East Side Pockets

Food: Middle Eastern

Address: 278 Thayer St

Phone: (401) 453-1100

Cool Features: They make it in front of you as you choose what goes in the pocket.

Price: $6 and under per person

Hours: Monday-Saturday 10 a.m.- 12 p.m.

Garden Grille

Food: Vegetarian

Address: 727 East Ave.

Phone: (401) 726-2826

Cool Features: A concocted smoothie called "The Crazy Weech"

Price: $12 and under per person

Hours: Sunday-Monday 4 p.m. – 12 a.m.

Geoff's

Food: Sandwiches

Address: 235 Thayer St., 163 Benefit St.

Phone: (401) 751-9214, (401) 751-2248

Cool Features:A sandwich that has every meat known to man on it.

Price: $6 and under per person

Hours: Sunday-Monday 8 a.m.-10 p.m

Meeting Street Cafe

Food: Sandwiches, Home Cooked Meals

Address: 220 Meeting St.

Phone:(401) 273-1066

Cool Features "Ginormous Cookies"

Price: $10 and under per person

Hours: Sunday-Monday 8 a.m.-11 p.m.

Mexico

Food: Authentic Mexican

Address: 948 Atwells Ave.

Phone: (401) 331-4985

Cool Features:Live mariachi band

Price: $6 and under per person

Hours: Monday-Thursday 10 a.m.-9 p.m., Friday-Saturday 10 a.m.-9:30 p.m., Sunday 11 a.m.-9 p.m.

Mill's Tavern

Food: American with a French influence

Address: 101 N. Main St.

Phone: (401) 272-3331

Cool Features: Nice atmosphere

Price: $25 and under per person

Hours:Sunday-Thursday 5-10 p.m., Friday-Saturday 5-11 p.m.

The Modern Diner

Food: Breakfast

Address: 364 East Ave

Phone: (401)726-8390

Cool Features: Eat in a real o d fashioned diner

Price: $6 and under per person

Hours: Monday-Saturday 6 a.m.-3 p.m., Sunday 7 a.m.-2 p.m

Sakura

Food: Sushi (Japanese)

Address: 231 Wickenden St.

Phone: (401) 331-6831

Cool Features: Sit on the floor Japanese-style, BYOB

Price: $10 and under per person

Hours: Sunday-Monday Noon-11 p.m.

Spike's Junkyard Dogs

Food: Hotdogs, every kind you can think of

Address: 273 Thayer St.

Phone: (401) 454-1459

Cool Features: If you eat a certain number, you get them all for free, but I wouldn't recommend trying it.

Price: $6 and under per person

Hours: Sunday-Tuesday 11 a.m.-1:30 a.m., Wednesday-Saturday 11 a.m.-2 a.m.

Best Pizza:
Fellini's

Best Breakfast:
The Modern Diner, Brickway

Best Wings:
Wings To Go

Best Healthy:
Garden Grille

Best Chinese:
Asian Paradise

Best Place to Take Your Parents:
Paragon, The Blue Grotto

Student Favorites
Sakura, Bombay Club, Spike's

Closest Grocery Stores:

Eastside Marketplace
165 Pitman St.
(401) 831-7771
Open Daily 8 a.m. – 10 p.m.

Super Stop and Shop
77 Reservoir Ave.
(401) 467-1092

Whole Foods Market
601 N Main St
(401) 621-2378

Did You Know?

It's a tradition around Halloween that the Met makes **Monster Cookies**.

- If you eat twelve hotdogs at Spike's, **they won't make you pay for them**.

- Johnny Rocket's has become a **harmless but amusing** biker hang out.

"There are excellent restaurants in the greater Providence area of all sorts: Indian-The Bombay Club, Japanese-Hakuri East, Seafood-Hemenway's, Italian-The Blue Grotto."

Q "Thayer St., Spikes, Mediterranean Cafés, Pizza, **it's all good."**

Q "Restaurants off campus are okay. **Antonio's Pizza is cheap, by the slice.** East Side Pocket has good falafel."

Q "Providence is full of **great restaurants of all types.** Antonio's and East Side Pockets are great for less money, and dinner at midnight. Then there are too many more expensive excellent places to mention."

Q "Kabob 'n Curry, the Creperie, Andreas, **all the Italian places on Federal Hill**, Paragon, are all great."

Q "There are a lot of fantastic restaurants around. Lucky Garden, a Chinese restaurant on Smith St., has great food and dim sum on weekends. I also like the little Thai restaurant located on Hope St. called Sawadee. **Lemi's Restaurant is my favorite.** It's where Reservoir Avenue is near Cranston. It serves great local Chinese food and is really cheap! Also King's Garden is a nice dim-sum eatery place. I don't recommend going to Dragon Phoenix for dim sum—it's terrible. Apsara, from what I heard, is a great Thai restaurant as well (located across the India Point bridge)."

Q "Gordito Burrito is **cheap and filling.**"

Q "**Sun and Moon Korean restaurant is decent**. Sakura Japanese restaurant is good but expensive."

Q "Restaurants off campus are **good but expensive.**"

Q "**Yummy!** Kabob and Curry and Meeting St. Café are my favorites."

The College Prowler Take On...
Off-Campus Dining

Although most RISD kids stick pretty close to school, there are still a surprising variety of restaurants that are cheap enough for students which can be found on Main St., Thayer St., and Wickenden St. Despite Providence's small size, there are a surprising number of unique restaurants in the area. For instance, Thayer St. is one long chain of restaurants and shops that spans several blocks in the heart of the Brown/RISD radius. In one block, students will walk past Indian, Mexican, Pizza, Mediterranean, and Middle Eastern food, all of which are small unique restaurants. In fact, other than the occasional McDonald's downtown, you might have to go outside Providence proper to find a chain restaurant.

Because Johnson and Wales has a culinary academy, there is a wealth of interest and innovation in the immediate area that is constantly replenished, and there are always new and interesting places popping up. There is also a large Asian population who feeds some of the best Asian and Indian restaurants in the area. Finally, the large Italian population makes Federal Hill a Providence version of Little Italy. Thrown into the mix are a few college-hangout places such as Meeting St. Café and Antonio's, and a few four-star gourmet places such as Pastiche, a dessert restaurant, and you've got an extremely rich and diverse selection to choose from. It's impossible to get bored, but it helps to have a car or a friend with a car if you want to get to some of the more out of the way places.

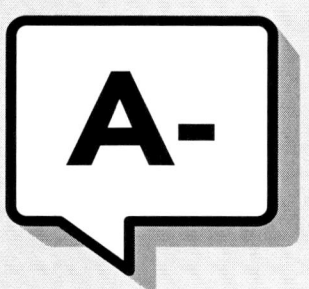

A-

The College Prowler™ Grade on

Off-Campus
Dining: A-

A high off-campus dining grade implies that off-campus restaurants are affordable, accessible, and worth visiting. Other factors include the variety of cuisine and the availability of alternative options (vegetarian, vegan, Kosher, etc.).

Campus Housing

The Lowdown On...
Campus Housing

Room Types:
Single (1 bed, 1 room)
Double (2 beds, 1 room)
Triple (3 beds, 1 room)
Suite (single or double rooms, shared lounge and bath)
Apartment Single (1 bed, 1 bath, 1 living room, 1 kitchen)
Apartment Double (2 bedrooms, 1 bath, 1 living room, 1 kitchen)
Apartment Triple (3 bedrooms, 1 bath, 1 living room, 1 kitchen)
Efficiency (1 bed/living room/kitchen/bath, tiny!)
Studio (1 bed/living room/kitchen/bath, small)

Room Types (continued):
Large Studio (1 bed/living room/kitchen/bath)

Best Dorms:
Colonial Apartments

Worst Dorms:
Farnum Hall

Students Living in:
Singles: 18%
Doubles: 63%
Triples/Suites: N/A
Apartments: 19%

Dormitories

Barstow House
62 Waterman St.
Floors: 3
Total Occupancy: 18 (+RA)
Bathrooms: 8
Co-Ed: Yes
Percentage of First-Year
Students: 0
Room Types: Singles, Doubles
Special Features: Studio Space,
TV Lounge, Kitchen, Laundry,
Brightly Painted Walls.

Carpenter House
1 Congdon St.
Floors: 3
Total Occupancy: 21 (+RA)
Bathrooms: 6
Co-Ed: Yes
Percentage of First-Year
Students: 0
Room Types: Singles, Doubles
Special Features: Studio Space,
TV Lounge, Kitchen, Laundry.

Colonial Apartments
175-185 Benefit St.
Floors: 3
Total Occupancy: 121
Bathrooms: 61
Co-Ed: Yes
Percentage of First-Year
Students: 0
Room Types: Efficiencies,
Studios, Large Studios, 2
Bedroom Apts., 3 Bedroom
Apts.
Special Features: Apartment-
style with personal kitchen,
living area, and bath,
communal laundry.

Congdon House
2 Congdon St.
Floors: 3
Total Occupancy: 31 (+RA)
Bathrooms: 10
Co-Ed: Yes
Percentage of First-Year
Students: 0
Room Types: Singles, Doubles
Special Features: Studio Space,
TV Lounge, Kitchen, Laundry,
Vending Machine, Porch.

Dexter House
Floors: 2 + Basement
Total Occupancy: 20 (+RA)
Bathrooms: 6
Co-Ed: Yes
Percentage of First-Year
Students: 0
Room Types: Singles, Doubles
Special Features: TV Lounge,
Laundry, Half Kitchen, Studio
Space, Porch, Vending
Machine, Connects to
Freshman Studio "What Cheer
Garage"

Dunnell House
16 Angell St.
Floors: 3
Total Occupancy: 16 (+RA)
Bathrooms: 6
Co-Ed: Yes
Percentage of First-Year
Students: 0
Room Types: Singles, Doubles
Special Features: Studio Space.
TV Lounge, Kitchen, Laundry,
House Ghost.

Dwight House
193-195 Benefit St.
Floors: 3
Total Occupancy: 21
Bathrooms: 21
Co-Ed: Yes
Percentage of First-Year Students: 0
Room Types: Studios, Large Studios
Special Features: Apartment-style with personal kitchen and bath, communal laundry.

East Hall
Floors: 4
Total Occupancy: 80
Bathrooms: 16
Co-Ed: Yes
Percentage of Men/Women: Unknown
Percentage of First-Year Students: 100
Room Types: Single and Double Suites
Special Features: Studio Space, TV Lounge, Kitchen, Laundry.

Farnum Hall
Congdon St.
Floors: 3 + Basement
Total Occupancy: 50
Bathrooms: 23
Co-Ed: Yes
Percentage of First-Year Students: 0
Room Types: Single Suites
Special Features: Studio Space, TV Lounge, Kitchen, Laundry.

Homer Hall
Floors: 6
Total Occupancy: 142
Bathrooms: 10
Co-Ed: Yes
Percentage of Men/Women: Unknown
Percentage of First-Year Student: 100
Room Types: Singles, Doubles
Special Features: Studio Space, TV Lounge, Kitchen, Ping Pong and Pool Tables, Vending Machines, Computer Station, Laundry.

Nickerson Hall
Floors: 6
Total Occupancy: 142
Bathrooms 10
Co-Ed: Yes
Percentage of Men/Women: Unknown
Percentage of First-Year Students: 100
Room Types: Singles, Doubles
Special Features: Studio Space, TV Lounge, Kitchen, Piano, Laundry.

Nightingale House
54 Prospect St
Floors: 3
Total Occupancy: 19 (+ RA)
Bathrooms: 8
Co-Ed: Yes
Percentage of First-Year Students: 0
Room Types: Singles, Doubles
Special Features: Studio Space, TV Lounge, Kitchen, Laundry.

Pardon Miller House

48 Angell

Floors: 3

Total Occupancy: 15 (+RA)

Bathrooms: 4

Co-Ed: Yes

Percentage of First-Year
Students: 0

Room Types: Doubles, Triples

Special Features: Studio Space,
TV Lounge, Kitchen, Laundry.

South Hall

Floors: 4

Total Occupancy: 80

Bathrooms: 16

Co-Ed: Yes

Percentage of Men/Women:
Unknown

Percentage of First-Year
Students: 100

Room Types: Single and
Double Suites

Special Features: Studio
Space, TV Lounge, Kitchen, Air
Conditioning, Laundry.

Thompson House

63 Angell St.

Floors: 3

Total Occupancy: 16 (+RA)

Bathrooms: 5

Co-Ed: Yes

Percentage of First-Year
Students: 0

Room Types: Singles, Doubles

Special Features: TV Lounge,
Laundry, Kitchen, Studio Space

Bed Type
Twin extra long, can be lofted upon request.

Available for Rent
Microwaves, Mini-Fridges

Cleaning Service?
In public areas and bathrooms quick clean, disinfect, and a vacuum are used usually every day in Outer Houses and dorms. No service in Colonial Apartments and Dwight.

What You Get
Bed, Bureau, Closet, Night Table, Desk and Chair, Internet Access, Lounge with Cable TV, Curtains, Wastebasket, Local Telephone Service.

Undergrads on Campus:
34%

Number of Dormitories:
12

Number of University-Owned Apartments:
2

Did You Know?

- All housing is **smoke free**.

- Dexter House **was a funeral home** in which H.P. Lovecraft's aunt had her wake.

- Dunnel House is supposedly **haunted by a young girl**.

Students Speak Out On...
Campus Housing

{ **"The freshmen dorms are really fun and the rooms are a fine size. There's enough space. If you're a party kid, go for Homer 5, for upper classmen, avoid Farnum."**

Q "The dorms are okay, but **you run into Public Safety too much."**

Q "East Hall is nice, **South is quiet**, Homer is smelly, Nickerson has bedbugs."

Q **"The dorms, freshmen especially, are uniformly awful.** Fake a medical condition to get a single…that's about al you can do to make it any better."

Q **"Nightingale House is horrible.** Colonial Apartments and Dwight Apartments are nice."

Q **"Our lottery system is inept.**

Q "Homer has its own lab, vending machine and pool and ping-pong tables. **Avoid Nickerson."**

Q "Being in the dorms is important because **you meet so many people**. I lived in school housing for three years and made a lot of friends and stayed connected to what was going on because of that. Dexter House and Colonial Apartments are great. I've gone through Farnum House and it scared me."

Q "The dorms were okay. I lived in Homer 2 and it wasn't as bad as I thought it would be. The only problem I had my Freshmen Year was the bathroom overflowed while I flushed it and dirty water spilled all over the place. That was an awful experience I will never forget. I think South has the nicest place since they have **air conditioning and individual suites with individual bathrooms.** I hung out in South 4 when I was a freshman. One thing I hated about freshmen dorms are the mice running around. They ate my Ramen noodles once and spat the Styrofoam pieces out and left their feces all over the place. I hated those nasty mice running around."

Q **"The dorms were fine**. Avoid Homer ground."

Q "Dorms are dorms. If you want to live in the lap of luxury, move off campus. It's hard enough to get housing as it is. They are average. **Not so new, but they function fine.** They were all pretty equal for the first year."

The College Prowler Take On...
Campus Housing

It's true; you can't avoid dorm life if you come to RISD as a freshman. However, there are some definite pluses to living in the quad. You are right by food and studios, and there are always people around and awake to hang out with. Some of the dorms are suites, so you're not sharing a bathroom with an entire floor, and all the rooms are big enough to be comfortable. If you're not so lucky as to get a suite, the communal bathroom is only for a year. Once you're out of the freshmen dorms, life gets better. Almost all of the dorms on campus are full of character and have a nice atmosphere and space to them. They are fairly small, so you get to know your house, and remain plugged into what's going on around campus without being smothered by it. If you stick it out a year or so in outer housing, then you will build up enough points to get yourself into Colonial Apartments, which is basically just as good as living off campus, only slightly less homey. Colonial is the goal of every student living on campus because you get your own bedroom and there is a bathroom and kitchen for every apartment.

Students who want to live in doubles or triples have an advantage because if one's partner gets a better lottery number, the best number of the group is what rules. For example, if one student has lived on campus for two years, and another has only lived on campus for one year, when the two-year student is called, she brings the one year student in to the room, they pick out their room together based on the floor plans, and both sign contracts in order to secure their space. If you are not present at the lottery, you will not be given a space, and there is no way to reserve a space. Often times, towards the end of the lottery, the spaces have been filled and students are left without housing. They may then join a waiting list, but usually only the top few students are taken. Bearing all this in mind, RISD is in the process of answering the shortage of student housing. A new housing facility at 15 Westminster Street is in the process of opening, and will be available to students for the 2005 school year. This housing will not be open to Freshmen, and now that there is enough space, RISD will require all Sophs. to live in school housing.

The College Prowler™ Grade on
Campus Housing: C-

A high Campus Housing grade indicates that dorms are clean, well-maintained, and spacious. Other determining factors include variety of dorms, proximity to classes, and social atmosphere.

Off-Campus Housing

The Lowdown On...
Off-Campus Housing

Undergrads in Off-Campus Housing:
66%

Average Rent for a Studio Apartment:
$550/month

Average Rent for a 1BR Apartment:
$700/month

Average Rent for a 2BR Apartment:
$1200/month

Popular Areas:
Benefit St., Wickenden St., Thayer St.

Best Time to Look for a Place:
End of Fall Semester, Wintersession

Assistance Contact:
Brian Janes, Director Residence Life

http://www.risd.edu/risd_housing/search_list.cfm

(401) 454-6651

Students Speak Out On...
Off-Campus Housing

"Living off campus is more of a hassle. They're building more housing for students and if you can get in, then go for it. It's very close."

Q "It takes some time to get the right place, but shop around because loads are available. **It's well worth it if you're close to campus.** Don't live far away or you will miss campus life and cool events."

Q "I'm not sure how convenient off-campus housing is, but it's worth it. You pay at least as much as you would living on campus, but it's much **nicer not to feel like you're living under surveillance,** and it's nice to get off campus a little. RISD doesn't have enough housing for even half the upperclassmen, so living off campus is the norm."

Q "It is worth it to **live off campus, if you can."**

Q "More campus housing is being built to accommodate students. **Landlords are crooks in Providence,** watch out!"

Q "A lot **depends on your landlord and how close you are to school**. It's important to start looking early, and try to rent from someone who you think takes care of their property."

Q "Off-campus housing is convenient, but **it's more expensive."**

Q "I definitely don't think living off campus is worth it. Although it may be $100 extra monthly for school housing, all utilities are included: heat, electricity, gas, as well as internet access. I heard **heating prices go way up during winter for off-campus houses,** and a lot of my friends paid so much money for heat, they had to turn it off even though it was freezing to lower their bills. Also there are a lot of sketchy landlords around Providence which one should try to avoid."

Q **"It can be a real pain in the butt**, but yes, it's worth it. I'm not the kind of person that likes to be looked after and policed. I like my space and I like to make my space mine."

Q "Off campus is farther, it takes energy to look for places, and landlords may screw you over. However, **it's cheaper, homier, you can bring a car**, and you feel like you're leaving school when you go home. That's been real important."

The College Prowler Take On...
Off-Campus Housing

Most students who live off campus swear that it's the only way to be, and those who are on campus note the convenience and proximity to school. Making the housing decision is something that every student to the present has had to face after Freshman Year. It's important to remember that one can enter the lottery, withdraw, and only loose a small deposit. Sometimes the safest idea is to consider both options, and then pick the best situation of the two.

Contrary to popular belief, it is generally cheaper to live off campus than in school housing. However, off-campus living costs can skyrocket if utilities are not included in the rent. Many students end up paying hefty heat bills in the winter, so it is important to talk to the previous tenants to get an idea of how the apartment is kept by the landlord, and what kind of bills to expect. Apartments that are within ten-minutes walking distance from the main part of campus, and that include heat in the rent, will be a much better deal, and a much more comfortable place to live, than school housing. It's true that some landlords are unscrupulous, but RISD has a lawyer service that will look over students' leases to let them know if they are being taken advantage of. Even though there is going to be more student housing available, off-campus housing is necessary for most RISD kids. If you are someone who's willing to shop around and be defensive about what kind of deal you are getting, then not only will you be fine, you'll probably live very happily and comfortably, with as much heat and utilities as you need. In many cases, it takes RISD just as long if not longer to get around to fixing little broken things than it does a real landlord. The downside is that the closer you want to be to campus, the more you'll have to pay.

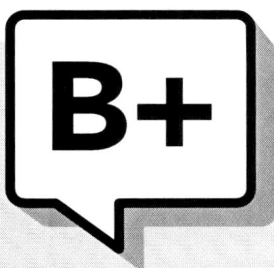

The College Prowler™ Grade on

Off-Campus
Housing: B+

A high grade in Off-Campus Housing indicates that apartments are of high quality, close to campus, affordable, and easy to secure.

Diversity

The Lowdown On...
Diversity

American Indian:
0%

Asian or Pacific Islander:
13%

African American:
2%

Hispanic:
5%

White:
68%

International:
11%

Unknown:
1%

Out of State:
90%

Political Activity:
Most kids are pretty liberal.

Most Popular Religions:
Christianity, Catholicism, Judaism

Gay Tolerance
Extremely Tolerant

Economic Status
Middle to Upper Class

Minority Clubs
The students on campus are integrated and all of the parties and events thrown by minority clubs are open to all students, not just those of the club. Some minority clubs include:

ACA (Asian Cultural Association)

Queer Student Union

Latin Alliance

Students Speak Out On...
Diversity

"The campus isn't that diverse. Black students have a poor representation."

Q "There are minimal black kids, but **plenty of Asians**."

Q "The campus is somewhat diverse. It's hard because there's **so little financial aid available for international students**. It's hard for any student that's not upper class."

Q **"RISD is very diverse.** Provided you consider white and Asian diverse."

Q "I guess diverse means Korean, Korean, Taiwanese, Korean, **Korean, Cuban, etc."**

Q "I think there might be **four black people, maybe five."**

Q "Gender wise, the female to male ratio is not as female dominated as I would have thought. Ethnically, there is diversity among international students although **more than half seem to be Korean."**

Q "The campus is only kind of diverse. It looks like it should be diverse, but most of the international students are Korean. **There's a wide cross-section of what part of the country the Americans come from**, but most of them are white."

Q "I think campus is very diverse, but I also feel like it's **becoming less diverse** because there's an overflowing amount of Korean students on campus. I think the school can work harder in terms of trying to get more people from various countries besides people from Korea (no offense against Koreans though, I have a lot of Korean friends!)"

Q "Campus is not very diverse. **There are lots of upper-middle to upper-class white kids**, lots of Asians, and a few sprinklings after that. I'd like to see more diversity."

The College Prowler Take On...
Diversity

Diversity at RISD is a tricky issue. It does not just call for non-white non-Americans; but a mixing of students from different backgrounds, socio-economic status, culture and race. The predominant theme that categorizes RISD is white, upper-middle class, Christian female. There is also a large population of Koreans on campus, and several other Asian ethnicities; but in general, there is not a whole lot of diversity. On the positive side, the diversity that does exist at RISD is made the most of, and most students benefit from learning about each other and how people from different cultures and artistic backgrounds approach art and design problems. Most studio classes are set up to allow all students in the class to participate in critiques. Everyone gives their input based on their personal backgrounds, aesthetics, and beliefs. By having a diverse range of students in these intimate situations, there is a great deal of aesthetic exchange, and many students are able to expand their understanding of what their art can be. Especially relevant conversations center on gender politics in art, cultural identity, and product design for a world market.

There are always continuous efforts to expand the diversity of students at RISD. Most recently, there was a special effort made in order to financially assist students coming from poorer countries. These small strides are fully supported and sometimes initiated by the students. As RISD continues to make it easier for students from different backgrounds to come together, the new mix of students will be welcomed with open arms. The international and minority students that are at RISD enrich all students' experiences and the students are happy to have each other.

The College Prowler™ Grade on

Diversity: C

A high grade in Diversity indicates that ethnic minorities and international students have a notable presence on campus and that students of different economic backgrounds, religious beliefs, and sexual preferences are well-represented.

Guys & Girls

The Lowdown On...
Guys & Girls

Men Undergrads:
35.5%

Women Undergrads:
64.5%

Birth Control Available?
Yes, free condoms provided by Health Services, Planned Parenthood.

Most Prevalent STDs on Campus
Herpes, Chlamydia

Percent of Students with an STD
Unknown

Social Scene:

Most students are friendly and fun-loving, but not terribly socially minded. Everyone loves to cut loose, some go to parties, some just chill with friends, but work always comes first. When the semester begins to get really stressful, you will notice people walking on opposite sides of the street, recognize each other, and then pretend that they didn't see each other. However, when the stress is off, especially during Wintersession and after graduation, well, that's when RISD kids tend to earn their wild reputations.

Hookups or Relationships?

Most girls date outside the school, and most relationships in general are fairly serious. There are not a lot of random hookups, especially after Freshman Year.

Best Place to Meet Guys/Girls:

The best places to meet people are in bars, on "the Beach", at parties, and in class. Because most studio classes are not simple lectures where everyone is staring front and quiet, people get to know each other quite well. Most relationships at RISD are fairly mature, they may be casual, but there are less instances of randomly "hooking up" probably because it's a small campus and people get to know each other. It's not that it doesn't happen, but there is less a feeling of people being nameless and faceless, and more accountability.

Dress Code

To each his/her own. Some students dress punk, some hippy, some preppy, some expensively, some scary, most vintage chic, all very unique. Something to keep in mind, this is an art school; during the day a lot of people are wearing clothes that are comfortable to do studio work in.

Did You Know?

Top Places to Find Hotties:
1. At the bar

2. Across the studio, when you're knee-deep in plaster and can't move

3. Back home (wherever that may be)

Top Places to Hookup:
1. Artists' Ball (where everyone's drunk and naked)

2. Electroflo (where everyone's drunk and dancing)

3. Johnson and Wales (where everyone's not from RISD)

Students Speak Out On...
Guys & Girls

"The guys and girls are hot, fun and smart. There are too many gay guys, bummer, but they make great friends. There are plenty of good girlfriends."

Q "Guys? **RISD is predominantly female**, completely so in some majors. I'm sure there are some hot guys out there. There are definitely lots of very attractive, stylish girls."

Q "Honestly, I think there's **a lot of beautiful guys and girls on campus,** and I think they're equally hot. There are probably more beautiful girls on campus than guys just because of the ratio. Unfortunately, there are practically no guys in the Textiles Department. If girls need to find guys, I would recommend going to Brown. I have a lot of guy friends on campus, but I see them more as good friends and not people to date."

Q "Guys are few and far between, but **the girls are hot**."

Q "**I'd be better off if I were a lesbian.**"

Q "**RISD is the sexiest place I've ever been**. Everyone is beautiful! It's shocking!"

Q "RISD **needs more cute straight guys.**"

Q "**The girls are great!** Hot! But I don't know about the guys."

Q "**Hot?** Not really."

Q "This is a **ridiculous question.** Anyone who bases their decision to attend on this deserves to end up somewhere where everyone has prominent birth defects that are difficult to politely stop staring at."

The College Prowler Take On...
Guys & Girls

It may sound like a lot of places, but it certainly doesn't sound like college: tons of young, beautiful women, surrounded by a small showing of fairly attractive, mostly gay men. That's art school. However, gay or straight, the RISD men are mostly kind, talented, and funny people, who, regardless of their other intentions, will gallantly offer to walk a girl home at night, no strings attached. Both the gay and straight dating scenes are vibrant and energetic, and there are plenty of clubs, bars, and coffeehouses for both depending on what kind of experience is desired. The women at RISD are smart, beautiful, and talented, and often dating at RISD is more inhibited by students' tight work schedules than by the students themselves.

The most important thing to remember at RISD is that it's personality that gets you the farthest. While there are some very beautiful women and some hot guys around, it's really all about the attitude. If you are unique and comfortable with yourself, you will become one of the sexiest students on campus. If personality didn't get you as far as you wanted, talent and dedication will pick up the rest. If you are looking for casual hookups, you can find them, but you may be better off going to Brown parties or to bars where Johnson and Wales kids hang out because the intensity that comes with being at RISD and surrounding yourself with art, usually transfers to intensity in relationships as well.

The College Prowler™ Grade on
Guys: C+

A high grade for Guys indicates that the male population on campus is attractive, smart, friendly, and engaging, and that the school has a decent ratio of guys to girls.

The College Prowler™ Grade on
Girls: B+

A high grade for Girls not only implies that the women on campus are attractive, smart, friendly, and engaging, but also that there is a fair ratio of girls to guys.

Athletics

The Lowdown On...
Athletics

Athletic Division:
Small Art School (Cooper Union is our biggest rival)

Men's Varsity Sports:
The Nads (ice hockey)

The Balls (basketball)

Women's Varsity Sports:

The Jugs (soccer)

Club Sports:
Soccer

Hockey

Basketball

Sailing

Bicycling

Rock Climbing

School Mascot:
Scrotie (7 ft. tall penis with balls and cape)

Getting Tickets

Most games are free and require no tickets. Every once in a while you might have to pay a dollar or two, but most times they give away prizes because they're grateful that someone actually showed up.

Most Popular Sports

Sprinting to class

Overlooked Teams

Architecture's mental gymnastics

Best Place to Take a Walk

Waterplace Park along the canal (when it's not dark out), Lincoln Woods, Newport Cliffwalk.

Gyms/Facilities

RISD Gym

RISD Gym is the only gym on campus. It has a small treadmill room, a room with nautilus machines and free weights, and a couple rooms for cardio/martial arts/dance classes. It's often crowded and the hours are restricted, but it's all ours.

Brown Gym

RISD students are allowed access to all Brown's athletic facilities including their Gym, Pool, Tracks, Ice Rinks, and weight rooms, provided that there is no schedule conflict with Brown sports teams.

Did You Know?

Students can participate in intramurals at Brown University; those sports include **Ultimate Frisbee, tennis, and softball.**

• The cheerleaders for the Nads wear the colors of **pink and black**.

Students Speak Out On...
Athletics

"Sports at RISD aren't big at all. I don't even know if they're fun, but they're definitely funny."

Q "Sports are **non-existent.**"

Q "Athletics aren't big, but fun. **Go NADS!**"

Q "Sports are NOT big at all. It's gotten better from the past. The biggest thing is probably ice hockey, the Nads, and maybe the Balls. Students are so busy getting their studio work done, **I don't think they have time to do extra-curricular stuff.** I tried fencing and Tai Chi on campus (organized by OSL) and I had a lot of fun."

Q **"How big are sports? Tiny."**

Q "Hmmm...I **don't think they're that big.**"

Q "**Athletics aren't very big**, unless you count getting drunk to cheer on a giant, foam, rubber penis a sport."

Q "Sports are non existent. **Some of them are fun clubs.** They're more like fun and loose get-togethers."

Q "Sports aren't so big—no time. **It's mostly for amusement purposes.**"

Q **"Athletics are fun-ish."**

Q **"Our cheers are: 'Support your Balls,'** and 'go nads, they're big.' I think that says it all."

The College Prowler Take On...
Athletics

While serious athletics is pretty much out of the question at RISD, students definitely have fun with what they've got. Imagine, during parents' weekend, half the campus drunk and yelling obscenities at a team of completely bewildered ice-hockey players while a giant penis in a cape leads cheers from the sidelines. Often the Jockstraps (cheerleading team) will rouse the RISD crowd into heckling some players so badly that fights ensue. Another rallying move is when Scrotie tries to ram the goalposts tip-first. (Some images really are worth a thousand words.) Once in a while there will be a scandal during which Scrotie has been kidnapped by an unnamed group. The ransom demands that all Nads players skate around the rink after the game in their underwear in order to retrieve their precious mascot. The following drawn-out drama will be involved and scandalous, in order to fill the stands. The Nads sometimes score on themselves, but on the off chance that you do see them win, it's not only a blast, but it's totally priceless to see the look on the other teams' faces. Nobody wants to get beaten by The Nads.

The Balls are a slightly different experience. There is no obscene mascot and profane cheerleading team, and most games appear to be fairly average, however the advertising is uniquely RISD. While walking across campus, you may encounter several posters of our beloved President Roger Mandle, nonchalantly cradling two basketballs to his chest, and solemnly urging the RISD community to "Support Your Balls". RISD sports? A for Amusement.

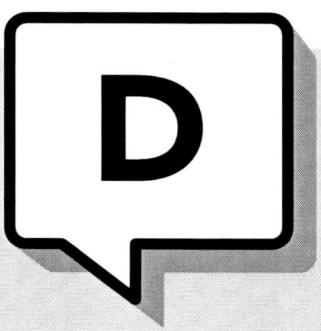

The College Prowler™ Grade on

Athletics: D

A high grade in Athletics indicates that students have school spirit, that sports programs are respected, that games are well-attended, and that intramurals are a prominent part of student life.

Nightlife

The Lowdown On...
Nightlife

Club and Bar Prowler:
Popular Nightlife Spots!

Club Crawler:

The local clubs are fairly standard, except for club Hell, which is anything but ordinary. Hell almost always has a theme, and the theme is usually amusing. Most clubs don't have a cover charge, or if they do, it's very minimal, and many clubs will let you in if you're eighteen and up.

Lupos at The Strand

79 Washington Pl.

(401) 751-2700

Hours dependent on scheduling of shows

Lupos is a one time concert venue turned club/concert venue as a result of the 2003 concert fire in Rhode Island. It can drag in some surprisingly big name bands, and usually the turn out is fair.

➡

Bar One

1 Throop Alley

(401) 621-7112

Dance Club open Tuesday-Sunday

Tuesdays are acoustic nights, DJs the rest of the week.

The Call & The Century Lounge

15 Elbow St. & 150 Chestnut St.

(401) 751-2255

Jazz and Blues hot spot.

DeVille's

148-150 Point St.

(401) 751-7166

Women-only club, open Tuesday-Sunday.

Hell

73 Richmond St.

(401) 351-1977

Open Tuesday-Sunday. Different nights have different themes, Sin Fest (Wed.), 80s Retro (Fri., 21+)

Hell is only for the brave at heart, lots of bondage, lots of dancing, lots of dressing up so that no one recognizes you. Hell hath no fury like 80's night.

Pulse

86 Crary St.

(401) 272-2133

Voted best gay club in Providence, theme nights Wed.-Sun. ranging from All-Male Review (Wed.) to "Phunky Fridays." Women's dance party Mermaids on Sat. nights.

Keg Room

101 Richmond St.

(401) 274-0170

Sports bar and Dance Club, 2 DJs, open Thurs.-Sat.

Bar Prowler:

There are a few bars around Providence that actually have very nice atmosphere. Many of these are a little more like European pubs and less like American dives. The nicest are The Wild Colonial and Custom House Tavern. One thing to keep in mind: if you want a cheap drink, buy yourself some beer at a liquor store. Most places charge $4+ for a shot or mixed drink. Another thing to keep in mind: Many liquor stores in Massachusetts and some in RI are open on Sundays.

Union Avenue Pub

306 Union Ave.

(401) 944-0450

Another one with nice atmosphere, Union Avenue is also a nice place to get a bite.

The Wild Colonial

250 S Water St.

(401) 621-5644

With stone walls and a dart board, The Wild Colonial is best when it's not very crowded, which is most of the time.

Fish Co.

515 South Water St.

(401) 421-5796

Inexpensive bar and grill, Wed. is college night.

Wickenden Pub

320 Wickenden St.

(401) 861-2555

Raffles and games, laid back and a little run-down.

Custom House Tavern

36 Weybosset St.

(401) 751-3630

A nice place for a drink, often has subdued, live music.

Trinity Brewhouse

186 Fountain St.

(401) 453-2337

Largest Brewery in RI, full menu, live music Wed.

Snooker's Café/The Green Room

145 Clifford St.

(401) 351-POOL

16 pool tables, and full bar, live acts in the Green Room

Useful Resources for Nightlife:

Providence@nightmagazine

Bars Close At: 1 a.m.

Local Specialties:

Newport Storms (beer bottled in Newport), Creepy Jason (rum, cherry coke, a dash of hot sauce, and a candy corn floating on top: please don't ask)

Primary Areas with Nightlife:

Downtown Providence

Cheapest Place to Get a Drink:

It's all just about the same.

What To Do If You're Not 21:

Almost all Bars have under-21 admissions on certain days, especially the trendier bars downtown that try to cater to the college crowd. Places like Bar One will card you at the door, and as long as you're over 18, you're welcome to stay and dance. If you're not into the bar atmosphere, there are usually a few parties around. Coffee and Teahouses also have great atmosphere, and are a great place to hang out with friends.

Starbucks

102 Waterman St.

(401) 273-8110

218 Thayer St.

(401) 421-1677

468 Angell St.

(401) 831-9481

Imagine, you can stand at the center, and going in almost any direction will take you to a Starbucks. Unless the direction you go in is to Coffee Exchange, which is recommended.

Coffee Exchange

207 Wickenden St.

(401) 273-1198

The coffee is gourmet and there's plenty of variety. There are also tons of beautiful baked goods.

Brewed Awakenings

5 Memorial Blvd.

(401) 421-2058

If half your group wants coffee, and the other half wants a beer, than you've come to the right place. It's not a full bar, but they do serve some bottled beers along with the coffee and bagels.

The Cable Car

204 S Main St.

(401) 272-3970

A definite favorite around campus, Cable Car is the only place where you can order a coffee or sandwich, and have them bring it to you as you watch an independent film while sitting on a couch.

Tealuxe

231 Thayer St

(401) 453-4832

The Starbucks of Teas.

Favorite Drinking Games:

Beer Pong

Card Games (A$$hole)

Century Club

Quarters

Power Hour

Organization Parties:

Many clubs, such as RISD Christian Fellowship or Asian Cultural Association, will throw food and movie parties, but there is no alcohol involved. There are three main organized parties that the school sponsors every year. The first is Artists' Ball, which comes around Halloween. The dress is "festive", which usually translates to "naked" and everyone makes their own costume. This is sometimes held in the convention center, sometimes downtown in the arcade, and centers around a lot of dancing and drinking. There is usually at least two DJs, and there's some food if you show up before ten thirty (which no one does). The second party is Electroflo during Wintersession, which is a scaled-down event, kind of like a rave. Some years it happens, others it doesn't. The last main event is the Beaux Arts Ball. This happens in the spring, and the dress is "formal or festive." This includes less nakedness, but still plenty of dancing, and it's usually held on the waterfront under a tent, which is very classy. There are cash bars at all events if you show ID.

Frats:

See the Greek Section!

Students Speak Out On...
Nightlife

"Parties are surprisingly not stupid. There are lots of good foods and drinks, smart conversation. As clubs go, the Strand gets good marks."

Q "Parties on campus? Bars and clubs? Most RISD students don't do a ton of partying/clubbing. I've heard of places downtown and apparently **there are always Brown keggers to crash."**

Q "I don't know how the parties are, **I don't drink."**

Q "Parties are fun, **themes and costumes are encouraged.** Stay away from trashy clubs on Thayer St. The dives on Wickenden are much better and cheaper. Watch out for Rough-Sesh!"

Q "There aren't parties on campus. Off campus, RISD parties have **a lot of drinking and dancing.** There are lots of great RISD dancing parties."

Q "The parties are good. **We stay away from the clubs** because they're filled with Johnson and Wales frat and sorority kids."

Q "I haven't been to too many parties, but **they seem to be pretty average."**

Q "Parties at RISD are usually pretty small. Probably **not more than thirty kids at the biggest.** There's a lot of drinking and a lot of music and talking and laughing. I rarely end up at a party where I don't know at least two-thirds of the kids there."

Q "Parties suck because no one is there to have fun. They can't forget about work. **Bars are more fun**."

Q **"There aren't many parties on campus.** Off campus, there are a number of bars and clubs ranging from 80's flashbacks (club Hell) to techno, to a relaxing drink in a calm atmosphere, like The Wild Colonial."

Q "It's nice because **you don't have to drink to have fun at parties here**. It's more about dancing and talking and stuff. There really aren't any parties on campus. It's pretty much not allowed so everything is more comfortable because it's in people's apartments."

The College Prowler Take On...
Nightlife

Most RISD kids go to parties instead of clubs and bars. Parties at RISD are in fairly small off-campus apartments, and usually involve a minimal amount of alcohol and a lot of dancing and dressing up. Because RISD is small, most kids know each other or have seen each other around and you will rarely end up at a party where you don't know anyone at all. Most parties only take place on Friday and Saturday nights, and many students only have time to go to one party in a week. On a Friday night, kids will start getting together around nine in the evening, and may hang out until four or so in the morning, but by mid-day Saturday, everyone is back in studio working. Most RISD parties are a lot of fun because when students do finally decide to take a break and cut loose, they do it in a big way. There are often theme parties such as "Cat and Mouse", "Playboy Party", "Black and White", and "Vintage Dinner Party". If kids are going out to have fun, 80's night is a favorite. In case you couldn't guess why, it's because they can get out their sweatbands and dress up.

The school parties are also pretty awesome; there is lots of dancing, lots of drinking, and lots of fun. Another great part about the nightlife in Providence is that there are things for those people under 21 to do. There are a bunch of coffee houses for people to hang out in, and most clubs let in those that are younger as long as they don't drink. Most people don't have a lot of time to party at night, but when they do, there is always something going on and the experience is always a memorable one.

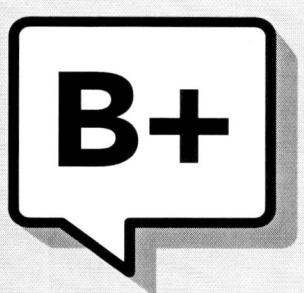

The College Prowler™ Grade on

Nightlife: B+

A high grade in Nightlife indicates that there are many bars and clubs in the area that are easily accessible and afforcable. Other determining factors include the number of options for the under-21 crowd and the prevalence of house parties.

Greek Life

The Lowdown On...
Greek Life

Number of Fraternities:
1

Number of Sororities:
1 (sort of)

Undergrad Men in Fraternities:
0%

Undergrad Women in Sororities:
.002 (five or seven people)

Sororities on Campus:
Psi Phi Pi

➜

Did You Know?

There have actually been three attempts within recent years to start Fraternities or Sororities. Oh, yeah, and **they've all been jokes**.

Students Speak Out On...
Greek Life

"Well, we kind of have a fake Sorority, Psi Phi Pi. But it's just funny. I don't think anybody around here could take something as stupid as frats too seriously."

Q **"NO GREEK LIFE!** BECAUSE!"

Q "Nope, **it's unoriginal.**"

Q "Some friends of mine made really terrible spanikopita one time. **I'm a big fan of Homer and Sophocles.** Actually I do think I know a Greek kid. He's named Kevin, he's from New Jersey. What? You mean all-male Hellenic social clubs? That sounds a little too homosexual even for us here at art school."

Q **"What on earth is a Greek life?"**

Q "I don't think the RISD community is big enough to actually have a Greek life. Also, I think **Sororities and Fraternities have a tendency to be exclusive.** I think there are enough drinking parties around campus (just in people's houses) that we don't need a frat. Also, RISD students are so busy with studio; I don't think we have time for that sort of thing. I think it's better if people join student clubs, since I personally find it more purposeful than joining a frat."

Q "I don't wish there was a Greek-life scene. Why would I? I've **never understood the whole Greek thing."**

Q "Sure, there could be a Greek life—**it would be fun.**"

Q "Oh, no! Greek life is **too forced and fake.** You should be able to have fun without the extra crap and peer pressure."

Q "There is no Greek life. People who are involved in Greek life are **mindless sheep who deserve to be eaten.**"

The College Prowler Take On...
Greek Life

It's no secret that RISD students revel in their uniqueness, and make fun of those who they perceive to be unable to think for themselves. While clearly many Fraternities and Sororities across the country are not the stereotypes that we all see in movies, to RISD kids, they might as well be. Psi Phi Pi exists because a group of friends thought it would be funny. They host parties, and make parodies of matching outfits, but that's about as far as it goes at RISD. If someone came into RISD and offered to set up the whole Greek system, there might not be enough interested students to fill one house.

Part of what kids are looking for when they come to art school is a community of students that do not buy into the systems of what is cool and what it means to belong in the same way that a more average college experience might provide. RISD students do not want to be labeled. They are independent thinkers who are not interested in the confines of closely associating themselves with a narrowed group of people. Students who are looking for a place to be social with people of similar interests need look no farther than their majors. It would not be unusual to see a group of students from Architecture hanging out in a bar by the BEB (Architecture building), or a gaggle of girls from Textiles chatting and drinking coffee in The Cable Car. The people RISD students work with and learn with become their closest friends, and school clubs and parties put them in touch with people not in their majors. That is all the community they need.

The College Prowler™ Grade on

Greek Life: D-

A high grade in Greek Life indicates that sororities and fraternities are not only present, but also active on campus. Other determining factors include the variety of houses available and the respect the Greek community receives from the rest of the campus.

Drug Scene

The Lowdown On...
Drug Scene

Most Prevalent Drugs on Campus:
Alcohol

Mmarijuana

Liquor-Related Referrals:
Under 20/year

Liquor-Related Arrests:
Under 5/year

Drug-Related Referrals:
Under 10/year

Drug-Related Arrests:
Under 5/year

Drug Counseling Programs
Yes. See Health Services

Students Speak Out On...
Drug Scene

"Some kids do tons of drugs, but it's not usually the kids you would expect. It's not in your face, but it's available."

Q "I have only seen some alcohol on campus during parties; however, **no one got very drunk.** There was lots of safe use."

Q "It's not a big thing here. There is drinking, but not as much as most other colleges. There are drugs too, but once again, not as much as many other places. I think most RISD people are too dedicated to their work to want to waste lots of time getting really messed up. **Caffeine abuse, that's rampant,** but everything else is limited."

Q "No comment—**I don't do drugs."**

Q "There's lots of pot, and a **decent amount of mushrooms."**

Q "There are **actually a lot of people taking drugs and also smoking.** I personally don't have contact with people who smoke up so I can't explain how serious the drug issue is. It's quite amazing how some people can handle drugs and still be able to keep up with their school work."

Q "There are **plenty to go around."**

Q "**It's not too out of reach for students,** but it's not really seen."

Q "There's **a lot more drinking than drugs**. Some pot is around but it's just not all over the place. People pretty much keep to themselves. I've never heard of anybody getting slipped something like a date-rape drug or anything."

Q "The drug scene is there, **if you do a little searching you can find most things.** It's not a problem, though. Most people here are too serious about what they do to be involved with it."

The College Prowler Take On...
Drug Scene

The drug scene at RISD is something that exists behind closed doors. It's definitely around, and if you look hard enough you can find what you want, but most people don't get mixed up in anything worse than pot, though there is some talk about the use of 'shrooms. You will not find yourself at a party with loads of coke lines on the table or bags of pot around with smoking circles in every corner. If there is some drug use at a party, unless you are participating, you probably won't even know about it because there are too many other students around dancing and talking without being under the influence of anything. Most students don't even recognize the use of any hard drugs on campus.

There is a manageable amount of drinking around, but for most people it's not for more than one night a week, if every week. There is also a small section of students who abuse caffeine and prescription drugs in order to stay awake and continue work, but mostly that's during finals. There is also a small population of people that smoke, but it isn't a major issue on campus. The bottom line is that students work too hard to distract themselves with a lot of drugs and drinking. What they do is too important to them to throw away, and those students who have been more into recreational use, find themselves failing because they can't keep up in class.

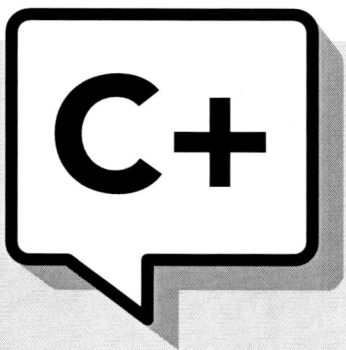

The College Prowler™ Grade on

Drug Scene: C+

A high grade in the Drug Scene indicates that drugs are not a noticeable part of campus life; drug use is not visible, and no pressure to use them seems to exist.

Campus Strictness

The Lowdown On...
Campus Strictness

What Are You Most Likely to Get Caught Doing on Campus?

Trying to stay in studio after the buildings close.

Students Speak Out On...
Campus Strictness

> **"Drinking is basically tolerated as long as you don't disturb people, but drugs are less tolerated. I know two people who were kicked out this year for smoking weed in the dorms."**

Q "If you live in the dorms, be discreet. Otherwise, I **don't think it's a problem."**

Q "It's weird because if you live in an outer house, **your house can vote to be a wet or dry house.** If the majority votes dry, you can get busted for having alcohol even if you're of legal age. If the house is wet, you are not allowed to drink in the presence of anyone under twenty-one. That's really the last nail in the coffin of enjoying a drink on campus."

Q "Campus police are **pretty strict."**

Q "I don't think it comes up that much. People caught drinking in the dorms **get a slap on the wrist**... technically there's no drinking in studio at all. Because most kids live off campus after Freshman Year outside the range of campus police, and everyone is so into their work, I don't consider it an issue."

Q **"If they catch you, you get 'written up.'** It's not a huge deal since most people live off campus."

Q "Policies are strict. **I've seen people get kicked out of housing**. I don't know if they kick you out of school, though."

Q "They let some things slip by—**too many screw ups and you get kicked out.**"

Q "They're pretty naive about it I think. **They're mostly unaware.**"

The College Prowler Take On...
Campus Strictness

The campus police are strict about some things and more lax about others, and it is especially dependent on which officer you run into. Usually, if a student is caught drinking or doing drugs on campus, they're given one more shot. In severe cases, campus officers have been more concerned for the student's wellbeing than in discipline. However, later these cases will probably still be brought to a disciplinary board and decided accordingly. The penalty is usually being kicked out of housing, but the administration has been known to expel some students.

The school is also known for its strictness when it comes to academic dishonesty, a.k.a. cheating; students risk penalties from the professor that catches them and a ruling made by the Academic Standing Committee, which, depending on the seriousness of the offense, can result in expulsion. What campus police are extremely strict on is getting everyone out of studio after the buildings close, and making sure that the monitored shops are closed at the appropriate times. This is an understandably important task because a sleepy student operating a table saw is clearly not safe, and it is the school's concern to be somewhat responsible for inhibiting tired students when operating dangerous machinery. This policy has been debated feverishly for several years. Students want 24-hour access, the school wants to save on resources and encourage students to sleep. Until the school caves, campus police will be patrolling, yelling at kids to get out, and locking doors. Overall, students find campus strictness to be fairly lax, and not something they are too concerned with.

The College Prowler™ Grade on

Campus Strictness: A-

A high Campus Strictness grade implies an overall lenient atmosphere; police and RAs are fairly tolerant, and the administration's rules are flexible.

Parking

The Lowdown On...
Parking

Approximate Parking Permit Cost
N/A

Common Parking Tickets:
Expired Meter: $15.00
No Parking Zone: $30.00
Handicapped Zone: $30.00
Fire Lane: $30.00
Overtime Parking: $15.00
Double Parking: $30.00

Student Parking Lot?
No

Freshman Allowed to Park?
No

Parking Services
N/A

Parking Permits

You may pick up a student parking permit for free from RISD Public Safety. These permits allow you to park in RISD lots between the hours of 7 p.m. and 7 a.m.

Did You Know?

Best Places to Find a Parking Spot
On Congdon St. after 10 a.m.

Good Luck Getting a Parking Spot Here!
The City of Providence.
P.S. There's no overnight street parking allowed.

Students Speak Out On...
Parking

> "Parking is non existent. Along with that non-space, if they declare a snow emergency, you have an hour or two to move your car before they tow it."

Q **"Parking is CRAZY.** There is far away parking only."

Q "There is **no parking**—not even for staff."

Q "There's no parking anywhere, and even though the tickets aren't that expensive, they add up like you wouldn't believe. If you don't pay your ticket or contest it within 14 days, it doubles, after 28 it triples. **If you accumulate too many unpaid tickets, they put the boot on your car,** or have it towed."

Q "We don't have a lot of parking space, so we see lots of people on bikes. Providence in general is **not the best place to park cars."**

Q "The parking is crappy. There's no parking anywhere—r**ide a bike."**

Q "The parking is horrible. **There's no student parking anywhere**. Even teachers have trouble. Streets are always packed and most places have no more than a two-hour parking limit. Car + Providence = tickets, tickets, tickets, unless you rent a space or leave your car at your apartment and walk to class."

Q "It's **extremely hard to find a spot.** Many of my friends got their car towed because they parked on the street several times. My friends don't normally drive to get to classes. A lot of students bike a lot. So biking is another good alternative."

Q "Do not park. **You will get towed**."

Q "The parking scene is horrible—**everyone gets ticketed**."

The College Prowler Take On...
Parking

Because the main part of RISD exists in the middle of Courthouses, Cafés and Office buildings, the places that would be available for parking are reserved for the business people and customers of those places until 5 p.m. on weekdays. Places that do not have this restriction only allow parking for one or two-hour intervals. Many students who have cars end up walking to and from class during the day. They then bring their cars back in the evening so they won't have to walk or take the shuttle late at night or early in the morning when they've finished in studio. For most students, this schedule is a pain, but is easily gotten used to.

What students can't become accustomed to is the amount of tickets received by those students who move too far away to walk. Meter maids watch your car like a hawk, and if you're in a one hour and you've been there for an hour and a half, expect something unfriendly in the near future. The irony of it all is that within the main part of Providence, unless you're talking four or five in the morning, street parking by the school is probably the easiest place to park. There are a few parking lots in the downtown area that are a five- to ten-minute walk from campus. However, these lots will probably charge you around $25 a day to park. Furthermore, if you are not done in studio until three in the morning, it may not be safe to walk downtown by yourself in order to retrieve your car. There are also one or two garages downtown where spaces are available for rent if you live on campus or in an apartment that does not include a parking space. Unfortunately, the same situation applies where having a car is not any better if you have to be unsafe in order to get to it. Just remember: walking is good for you.

The College Prowler™ Grade on

Parking: D

A high grade in this section indicates that parking is both available and affordable, and that parking enforcement isn't overly severe.

Transportation

The Lowdown On...
Transportation

Ways to Get Around Town

On Campus
RISD/Brown SAFERIDE
Monday-Friday 5 p.m.-3 a.m.

(401) 863-1778

SAFERIDE will take a student from one place on campus to another, or from their off campus house to campus, and from campus to their off campus house.

Public Transportation
Bus/Trolley

Rhode Island Public Transportation Association (RIPTA), (401) 781-9400

265 Melrose St.

Schedules available online and in the Office of Student Life

Taxi Cabs

Airport Budget Cab (401) 453-4851

Airport Express (401) 521-4200

Arrow Cab Co. (401) 946-5333

Checker Cab (401) 273-2222

Economy Cab (401) 944-6700

Providence Cab Co. (401) 521-4200

Yellow Cab (401) 941- 1122

Car Rentals

Avis, local: (401) 736-7500; national: (800) 831-2847, http://www.avis.com

Budget, local: (401) 751-5401; national: (800) 527-0700, http://www.drivebudget.com

Dollar, local: (401) 739-8450; national: (800) 800-4000. http://www.dollar.com

Enterprise, local: (401) 861-4408; national: (800) 736-8222, http://www.enterprise.com

Hertz, local: (401) 274-4043; national: (800) 654-3131, http://www.hertz.com

Rent-A-Wreck: (401) 454-1234; national: (800) 944-7501, http://www.rentawreck.com

Best Ways to Get Around Town

RIPTA Buses

RIPTA Trolley

Bike

Car

Walk

Shuttles:

RISD provides school sponsored shopping shuttles that go to Target, Home Depot, the Asian market, Savers, and the Recycling Center nearly once a week.

Ways to Get Out of Town

Airport

Providence T.F. Green

2000 Post Rd., Warwick

(401) 737-8222

(888) 268-7222

http://www.pvdairport.com

T.F. Green is a ten to fifteen minute drive from school.

Logan International Airport

Boston

(800) 23-LOGAN

http://www.massport.com/logan

Logan is about an hour drive from school.

How to Get to the Airport

Airport Limousine Shuttle

(401) 737-2868

http://www.airporttaxiri.com/schedule.html

The shuttle stops in front of 30 Waterman (Freshman Quad) and takes about 30 minutes to get to the airport. It stops twenty-five minutes after the hour, every hour from five a.m. until 11 p.m. and costs $9 per person.

➜

A Cab Ride to the Airport
Costs: $28.00 including tip

Airlines Serving Providence:

American Airlines,
(800) 433-7300,
www.americanairlines.com

Continental, (800) 523-3273,
www.continental.com

Delta, (800) 221-1212,
www.delta-air.com

Northwest, (800) 225-2525,
www.nwa.com

Southwest, (800) 435-9792,
www.southwest.com

TWA, (800) 221-2000,
www.twa.com

United, (800) 241-6522,
www.united.com

US Airways, (800) 428-4322,
www.usairways.com

Greyhound
1 Kennedy Plaza
(401) 454-0790
www.greyhound.com
Bonanza Bus Lines
1 Bonanza Way
(888) 751-8800
www.bonanzabus.com

Amtrak
Amtrak/MBTA Station
100 Gaspee St.
(800) USA-RAIL
www.amtrak.com

Travel Agents
Providence Travel Inc
229 Thayer St.
(401) 521-4545

Students Speak Out On...
Transportation

"Transportation isn't very convenient, but no one has time anyway. There are plenty of shopping shuttles that students use, but most no one has the time to go too far."

Q "The trolleys are okay, but the **buses are a mystery to me.**"

Q "Public transportation is not that convenient. **SAFERIDE needs to be better.**"

Q "The public transportation is **pretty convenient.**"

Q "**We need rent-a-bike** or u-haul on campus."

Q "It takes a while for me to wait for buses and trolleys. I think **a car is necessary for living off campus**, and if you need to go grocery shopping or buying materials for classes. But unfortunately, there's not a lot of parking space on RISD campus."

Q "I haven't used them much but the **trolleys and buses seem pretty easily available.**"

Q "It's a small city so **most people walk or bike around.** If you need to take the bus or trolley, they're around."

Q "**Buses have weird schedules here** and are kind of difficult to figure out. The trolley is easy to catch but only runs through historic Providence. Both stop running pretty early."

Q "**Providence transportation is confusing**, but SAFERIDE's easy enough."

The College Prowler Take On...
Transportation

Oftentimes students will take the RIPTA Trolley up the hill, or from one end of Benefit St. to the other. This provides a convenient and quick way to get where they're going. Past that, things get a little hazy. The buses are slightly confusing, and schedules are not well posted. In order to get to the fabric store, a student must take around five transfers. There had been some discussion about giving RISD students the popular deal where they may show their IDs and ride for free, but the fact of the matter is, free or not, there are not a lot of kids willing to get on a bus bound for an unknown destination.

Providence is so small that the parts that most people want to get to are easily within walking or biking distance. Most people only take the buses if they want to go to Newport or somewhere else outside the city. For Boston, or NY, the train is the most efficient. The places that are hard for students to reach are places like Home Depot or Jo-Ann Fabrics, in order to get supplies for projects. Also, in relation to the school, the nearest real grocery store is walk-able, but not pleasantly walk-able, especially when carrying tons of food. Except for these few places that students have access to with the RISD shopping shuttles, there's not a lot that's worth going to outside the walkable Providence radius.

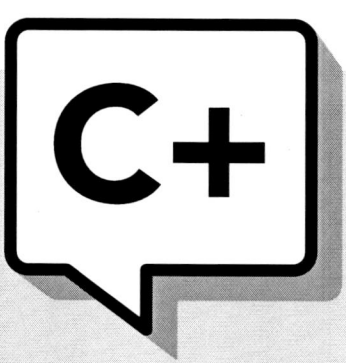

The College Prowler™ Grade on

Transportation: C+

A high grade for Transportation indicates that campus buses, public buses, cabs, and rental cars are readily-available and affordable. Other determining factors include proximity to an airport and the necessity of transportation.

Weather

The Lowdown On...
Weather

Average Temperature
Fall: 54 °F
Winter: 31 °F
Spring: 49 °F
Summer: 71 °F

Average Precipitation
Fall: 3.93 in.
Winter: 4.0 in.
Spring: 4.75 in.
Summer: 3.48 in.

Students Speak Out On...
Weather

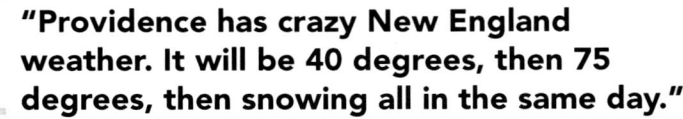

"Providence has crazy New England weather. It will be 40 degrees, then 75 degrees, then snowing all in the same day."

Q "It's very variable: **hot, humid, cool, breezy, freezing, wet, dry."**

Q "**You'll need all sorts of clothes:** good boots, good rain gear, jacket or umbrella."

Q "The weather is **rainy until it snows."**

Q "My roommate freshman year was from California, and when she whipped out the heavy coat in late September, I thought she was really going to be in for it. If you're not expecting what I consider subtropical weather, than Providence is fine. I grew up in Ohio and let me tell you, Providence is nearly the same only it's sunnier, milder, the snow doesn't stay on the ground as long, and it doesn't rain everyday. I really **don't know what people are complaining about."**

Q "The weather is kind of depressing. **I wish there was more sunlight!** Summer is really wonderful, though. Definitely bring long-sleeved t-shirts."

Q "**It rains quite often**, but you can wear basically anything."

Q "**Every winter is deemed 'the coldest winter ever'.** It's in the negatives."

Q **"Providence has cold, long winters**. Dress in layers because the studios are hot. Get good shoes for walking up the hill."

Q "The weather is **great because I like the cold."**

Q **"Weather is very inconsistent**. It can get very warm sometimes and an hour later it might be snowing. So students should bring all sorts of clothing from t-shirts, tank tops, to heavy duty snow coats and leg warmers. I had a senior friend who once wore a ski mask around, because of the chilling winds during the winter."

Q "The weather's New England. **It never gets extremely hot,** but the winters are cold; you'll need lots of sweaters, and gloves."

The College Prowler Take On...
Weather

If you can see yourself getting excited about a New England Fall, then Providence is probably just right for you. It's true that the winters can be a little harsh, and it definitely rains a lot, but the winters are slightly milder than Boston, not as windy as Chicago, and probably more interesting than the season-less experience of California or Florida. The most frustrating aspect of Providence weather is its inconsistency. One day it will be unseasonably warm, and the next it will snow. However, this means that the snow doesn't stay on the ground for very long because as soon as it snows, the weather warms again.

Providence summers are ideal because they don't get too hot, and usually summer, spring and fall are very sunny and pleasant when it's not raining. The fall foliage gives a nice atmosphere, and while it may be a little chilly out, the air usually smells crisp and clean. It's important to bring lots of layers because most buildings are kept very hot in the winter, and students will cook in their heavy-winter clothes. Remember to get into the spirit; there are plenty of good sledding hills around. But it is important to remember that winter isn't the only season Providence has. The beginning of fall and spring tend to be rainy, but the beginning and end of the school year tend to be bright and sunny. Rhode Island has over 400 miles of beaches, so students recommend bringing flip flops and bathing suits for this time of the year.

The College Prowler™ Grade on

Weather: C

A high Weather grade designates that temperatures are mild and rarely reach extremes, that the campus tends to be sunny rather than rainy, and that weather is fairly consistent rather than unpredictable.

Report Card Summary

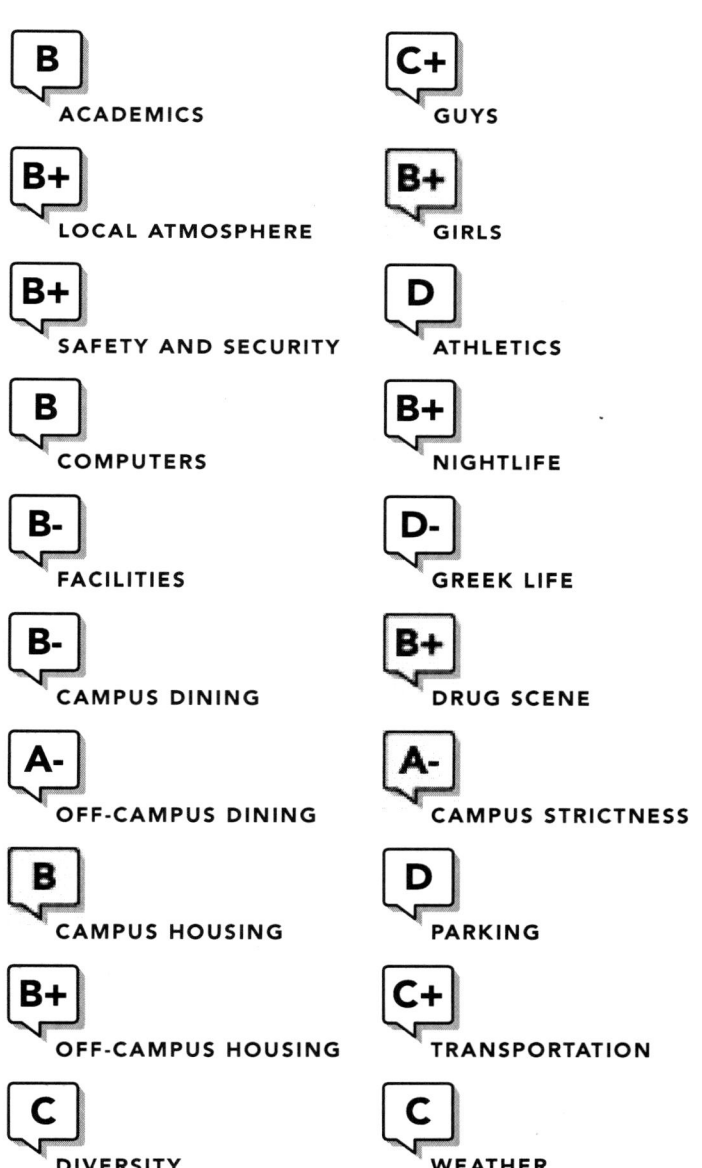

B ACADEMICS

C+ GUYS

B+ LOCAL ATMOSPHERE

B+ GIRLS

B+ SAFETY AND SECURITY

D ATHLETICS

B COMPUTERS

B+ NIGHTLIFE

B- FACILITIES

D- GREEK LIFE

B- CAMPUS DINING

B+ DRUG SCENE

A- OFF-CAMPUS DINING

A- CAMPUS STRICTNESS

B CAMPUS HOUSING

D PARKING

B+ OFF-CAMPUS HOUSING

C+ TRANSPORTATION

C DIVERSITY

C WEATHER

Overall Experience

Students Speak Out On...
Overall Experience

"It's been a good one. There have been downsides, things I didn't enjoy, but nothing I think I could have necessarily avoided by going anywhere else (all the dorms I've seen are equally crappy)."

"I love it—I **wouldn't want to be anywhere else.**"

"RISD is a school that is **academically and personally rigorous** and challenging."

"**RISD is great, sometimes**. But here is where I want to be for the opportunities."

"Generally, I love my school, but **I miss home.**"

Q "Art school is the biggest joke and the best thing ever. **Don't take it too seriously.**"

Q "I love it here. There are problems, but there are problems everywhere. **My class is amazing!**"

Q "I love RISD and I can't imagine being in another school. Everyone is so nice and friendly. You can talk to random people out of your major and feel perfectly comfortable talking to them. **I was amazed at how much talent people have** and how much you can learn from each other. It's very inspiring to be around a group of talented people, you get new ideas from your peers. I have also branched out a lot, and have many friends from other departments. I find it comforting to hang out with people from ID or Illustration or FAV or Architecture because they give you another perspective of how art can be done, and how their departments function. I also gained a great experience involving myself with extracurricular activities. It trained me to think beyond RISD, and outside of RISD. Also I learned a lot of leadership skills being involved with various activities."

Q "I think I'm meant to be here. Despite a couple of minor drawbacks, **this school has helped me hone my technical knowledge** and fine-art capabilities. A number of teachers have been life-alteringly inspirational. It is an intense place and I don't recommend attending unless you bring that same level of intensity to the table."

Q "I like this school very much. But I wish my major were five years because **I didn't quite learn enough in four years.**"

The College Prowler Take On...
Overall Experience

Many students love and hate RISD at the same time. The workload may be extremely demanding, but RISD students are not coming to receive the typical college experience. They are coming to get in touch with a community of artists that will enrich their understanding of art as a medium. Students who come to RISD are coming to gain access to an amazing amount of resources and equipment, which enable them to push their art form as much as possible. Students who come to RISD aren't looking for the big party school or a Greek scene, they are coming here to find themselves, to be individuals, and excel in their individual talents.

RISD students work very hard, and are rewarded in the end. Many feel they are prepared to enter some sort of job, or pursue a way to become active professionals in their field. In many ways RISD is like boot camp for art, but it's also an amazing opportunity for students to make the work that they want to make and learn about themselves and their surroundings in the process. Once students let go of any ideas of what college is supposed to be, they will realize that what RISD offers is not only a completely unique and exhilarating experience, but a degree that holds a lot of weight in the professional world, and skills that will serve the students for their entire lives. If you ask any student at RISD, they will say that as much as they complain, they would never go anywhere else.

The Inside Scoop

The Lowdown On...
The Inside Scoop

RISD Slang

Know the slang, know the school. The following is a list of things you really need to know before coming to RISD. The more of these words you know, the better off you'll be.

The Beach: The patch of grass on the corner of Waterman St. and Benefit St.

Emo: Self-pitying and emotional

Pomo: Meaninglessly Trendy, Post-Modernist

Things I Wish I Knew Before Coming to RISD

- Only some majors offer the prospect of job stability.

- Sometimes following your gut is more important than listening to professors' specific opinions.

- It's not that easy to find the time to get up to Boston or down to New York.

- Coffee Drinking is necessary.

- Some majors are very definitely oriented towards design, while others are oriented towards fine art.

- If you want to work in a medium other than your major, you'll need a friend in that major to help you.

- It is important to be self-directed because advising is lax and you have to look after yourself.

Tips to Succeed at RISD

- Be Yourself!

- Learn to love coffee.

- Don't wait for crossing lights, just go.

- Get good walking shoes.

- Confidence is key (a lot of people end up inhibiting themselves when they could be expanding themselves).

- You have to fail along the way, and if you stop failing, you'll never get to the point beyond.

RISD Urban Legends:

- RISD is super haunted; here is where the haunts are and what they're doing:

Dunnel House- In the basement, a spirit knocks over trash cans, plays with the light fixtures and television, and brings chills to anyone in the room. On the back stairwell of the second floor a woman looks through the window.

Farnum Hall- Students report apparitions standing over their beds at night and hearing people whispering and walking through the halls when no one is there.

Homer Hall- On the fourth floor, a male ghost likes to be seen in the bathroom, and often changes music selections and breaks windows. Also on the fourth floor, a female turns on faucets. On the ground floor, the T.V. and VCR turn on and off on their own, an old man wanders the halls during all hours of the day, and another ghost bangs on the doors of the passageway between Homer Hall and Nickerson.

Nightingale House- The ghost likes to move furniture and play with the electricity.

Pardin Miller House- Two young children are often heard in the basement, and a woman's voice can often be heard.

- If you fall into the canal, it will dissolve your skin.

- Crooked former Mayor, Buddy Cianci, and RISD President, Roger Mandle, are like bread and butter.

- In connection with the mob activity and Cianci, there was a body found downtown without its thumbs.

- There are Billboards in Korea advertising RISD.

School Spirit

School spirit at RISD is alive, but in its own way. If you look around, you'll see a few students wearing school sweatshirts, or more commonly, NADS and BALLS shirts (because they're suggestive). People are here because they want to be, and they love the school, but they're sarcastic and cynical, and that's also part of the spirit. There is Scrotie, our penis mascot, and the Jockstraps (the cheerleading squad) wearing their pink and black spandex uniforms, that keep our ice hockey games fun and entertaining; especially when you have an entire crowd yelling out, "Go Nads!" For students and the administration, this type of humor is accepted and is a part of our school spirit.

Traditions

Cross-city pillow fight. Yep, you heard right. It may not be a long-standing tradition, but many think it's here to stay. For the last few years, students have managed to hold a giant pillow fight twice a year that travels from one place of meeting, through the city (and once the Providence Place Mall) to the canal. People come armored and armed, and ready for the beating to begin. It's usually fairly harmless because there aren't that many students that participate, and nearly no bystanders get caught in the middle, but it's always broken up by the police, even though no one gets sighted.

- There is a piece of grass known as the RISD Beach at the intersection of Waterman, Benefit, and Angell St. The spot earned its name because it has been a popular spot for students to sun bathe for over 50 years.

- Each year, since 1988, ceramics students have been contributing to a mosaic in the Quad's inner courtyard by adding new tiles.

- While most schools have traditional class rings, in 1994, Tamara Mottl designed the RISD ring which students now wear proudly.

- Each fall since 1966, new juniors and seniors from the European Honors Program venture off to Rome to study art and architecture.

Finding a Job or Internship

The Lowdown On...
Finding a Job or Internship

The ease of finding a job or internship comes at the mercy of one's major. Those in the design majors have an immediate one up on the fine arts majors, but don't count the latter out. The main thing working in RISD students' favor is that a degree from RISD carries a lot of weight. Whether you're applying for a corporate job in Architecture, or assistant to the head potter in a ceramics studio, when most employers hear that you are from RISD, it gets your foot in the door. One of RISD's shining attributes is that it works very hard to prepare its students for careers, and there are a lot of programs in place that give students access to invaluable information, whatever their major.

- RISD Alumni and Career Services heads up most of the effort to find students and alumni internships, jobs, and information. They have a constantly updated database that may be searched for jobs or internships, based on your student status, major, and location. You may also make an appointment for more acute counseling. Alumni and Career Services also provides a seminar and workshop series which provides sessions for nearly every students' situation. These lectures are free, and include programs such as: "Prospering as a Creative Entrepreneur," and "The Art of Business," and include topics such as: how to prepare a resumé and portfolio, interview tips for design students, how to start one's own fine art studio, how to start and run one's own gallery or business. . . the list goes on.

- The third piece in a RISD student's struggle to find employment rests with the curriculum of the major. Many majors have a class called "Professional Practice", which is designed to aid students in assembling their portfolio, resumé, and interview skills, and then puts those students in contact with companies or individuals in the field. If students are not hired by these companies directly, they learn a great deal about the process of applying for a job and what will be expected of them, as well as what types of working environments exist in their fields, and where these jobs are.

- The most recent employment poll is of RISD 2002 graduates. About 94% are currently employed, and another 4% are in some sort of full-time graduate school program. Out of those that are employed, 64% are employed in career fields directly related to their major, and 25% are in fields indirectly related to their major.

Advice:

The most important thing in finding a job or internship is one's portfolio, and the second most important thing is a student's connections. It's important to keep in touch with your department head, and see if she knows of jobs in the field that may be a good fit for you. Document your work as you progress through school so that you have a body of work to edit during your senior year.

Career Center Resources & Services

Alumni and Career Services
52 Angell St.
Hours: 8:30 a.m. - 4:30 p.m.

Offers, counseling services, career programs, departmental presentations, job and internship databases, online portfolio hosting, and a virtual career library.

To schedule an appointment to with a Career Counselor (401) 454-6614.

Grads Who Enter Job Market Within 1 Year of Graduation:
89%

AVERAGE SALARY INFORMATION

RISD doesn't actually collect salary information for each individual major. There is also a fairly wide disparity on what the general starting salary is because so many people go off to work on their own and set up their own businesses, while other work for large corporations or firms. What is evident is that with either path graduates choose, the average starting salary is consistently higher than the published salaries of other liberal-arts graduates one year after graduation.

Alumni

The Lowdown On...
Alumni

Website:
- intranet.risd.edu/departments/alumni.asp
- intranet.risd.edu/departments/default.asp?department=Alumni_Network

Office:
Alumni House
52 Angell St.
Phone: (401) 454-6620
Fax: (401) 454-6616
Hours: 8:30 a.m. - 4:30 p.m

Alumni Publications
RISD Views

Services Available:

Career Services aids in the career counseling of alumni using the same databases as the students. There are also 30 regional and local chapters of the Alumni club which help alumni stay in touch with one another, and sponsor programs and events. Specific services for alumni include career programs, resources on and off campus, and an active Alumni Association.

Major Alumni Events

RISD by Design Weekend (also parents' weekend) during which the Fall Alumni sale takes place. During this weekend, several presentations are set up for Alumni, and they may walk through and visit their old friends and department buildings. This is also an opportunity for them to gain exposure and sell some of their work. A portion of Benefit St. is closed off and lined with tables of Alumni work for sale. People come from all over to look and shop.

Did You Know?

Famous RISD Alumni:

Dale Chihuly

Scott MacFarlane

David Macaulay

Liz Collins

Mark Pollack

Martin Mull

David Byrne (dropped out)

Chris van Allsburg

Student Organizations

All clubs individual sites can be found at http://intranet.risd.edu.

AIAS Student Chapter
Anime Culture
Asian Cultural Association
The Balls
Bicycle Adventure
Blackletter
Blend
RISD Christian Fellowship
RISD Film Society
RISD Global
Graduate Student Alliance
RISD Jew Crew
Korean Christian Club
Korean Student Alliance
Latin Alliance
Mixed Media
Mountain Biking
RISD Musicians

The Nads
Network for Intellectual and Artistic Exchange
Pagan Society
Queer Student Union
Recycling
Reformed University Fellowship
Rock Climbing
Sailing
Skiing
Soccer
South Asian Student Association
Student Alliance Association
Student DJs
Student Gallery
Swing
Transportation Design Club
RISD Volleyball

BEST & WORST

The Ten BEST Things About RISD:

1	The Training and skill building
2	The Art Community
3	The Professors
4	The Museum
5	The Studio Facilities
6	How it prepares students to make a living at art
7	Connection with Brown
8	Guest Lecturers
9	Student Shows
10	Student Sarcasm/Sense of Humor

The Ten **WORST** Things About RISD:

1 Never Sleeping

2 The Lack of Financial Aid

3 The Lack of Interdepartmental Connections

4 The Timid Social Scene

5 Some Liberal Arts are Wishy-Washy

6 The Lack of Participation in Extra-Curricular Activities

7 The restricted resources that come with a small, private college

8 Most people think art school = 2 year program

9 Only a percentage of students will get paid for how hard they work

10 Enduring the horrible mispronunciations. (It's RIZ DEE, not RISSS DUH, not RYZE DUH, not RIZZED.)

Visiting RISD

The Lowdown On...
Visiting RISD

HOTEL INFORMATION

Biltmore Hotel
(401) 421-0700
11 Dorrance St.
Providence, RI 02903

The Westin, Providence
(401) 598-8000
1 W Exchange St.
Providence, RI 02903

Courtyard Marriott, Downtown Providence
(401) 272-1191
32 Exchange Terrace
Providence, RI 02903

Sportsman's Inn Inc
(401) 751-1133
122 Fountain St.
Providence, RI 02903

→

Take a Campus Virtual Tour:

http://www.risd.edu

To Schedule a Group Information Session or Interview:

Call admissions at (401) 454-6300 during business hours on weekdays in order to schedule an appointment. Group information sessions are offered 1:00 p.m. on Wednesdays and Fridays throughout the year.

Campus Tours:

Student-guided campus tours follow each group information session, and last approx. one and a half hours.

Overnight Visits:

There are no overnight visits prepared for prospective students.

Directions to Campus

Driving from the North
- Take I-95 South to the US-6 W/RI-10 exit- Exit 22 C-B-A toward Downtown/Providence Place

- Merge onto Memorial Blvd. via Exit 22A on the left toward downtown.

- Turn left onto Washington Place

- Washington Place becomes Waterman St.

- Turn left on Prospect St.

- Admissions is at 62 Prospect St.

Driving from the South
- Take I-95 North until you merge onto Memorial Blvd via Exit 22A toward downtown.

- Turn left onto Washington Pl.

- Washington Pl. becomes Waterman St.

- Turn left onto Prospect St.

- Admissions is at 62 Prospect St.

Driving from the East
- Take US-44 West to I-495 North toward RT-24/Boston

- Merge onto I-95 South via Exit 13B toward Providence

- Take the US-6 W/RI-10 exit-Exit 22C-B-A-toward Downtown/ Providence Place

- Merge onto Memorial Blvd. via Exit 22A on the left toward Downtown

- Turn left onto Washington Pl.

- Washington Pl. becomes Waterman St.

- Take a left on Prospect St.

- Admissions is at 62 Prospect St.

Driving from the West

- Take US-6 East toward Providence
- Take the exit toward Providence Downtown
- Merge onto Memorial Blvd.
- Turn left onto Washington Pl.
- Washington Pl. becomes Waterman St.
- Turn left on Prospect St.
- Admissions is at 62 Prospect St.

Words to Know

Academic Probation – A student can receive this if they fail to keep up with their school's academic minimums. Those who are unable to improve their grades after receiving this warning can possibly face dismissal.

Beer Pong / Beirut – A drinking game with numerous cups of beer arranged in a particular pattern on each side of a table. The goal is to get a ping pong ball into one of the opponent's cups by throwing the ball or hitting it with a paddle. If the ball lands in a cup, the opponent is required to drink the beer.

Bid – An invitation from a fraternity or sorority to pledge their specific house.

Blue-Light Phone – Brightly-colored phone posts with a blue light bulb on top. These phones exist for security purposes and are located at various outside locations around most campuses. If a student has an emergency or is feeling endangered, they can pick up one of these phones (free of charge) to connect with campus police or an escort service.

Campus Police – Policemen who are specifically assigned to a given institution. Campus police are not regular city officers; they are employed by the university in a full-time capacity.

Club Sports – A level of sports that falls somewhere between varsity and intramural. If a student is unable to commit to a varsity team but has a lot of passion for athletics, a club sport could be a better, less intense option. If a club sport still requires too much commitment, intramurals often involve no traveling and a lot less time.

Cocaine – An illegal drug. Also known as "coke" or "blow," cocaine often resembles a white crystalline or powdery substance. It is highly addictive and dangerous.

Common Application – An application that students can use to apply to multiple schools.

Course Registration – The time when a student selects what courses they would like for the upcoming quarter or semester. Prior to registration, it is best to have an idea of several back-up courses in case a particular class becomes full. If a course is full, a student can place themselves on the waitlist, although this still does not guarantee entry.

Division Athletics – Athletics range from Division I to Division III. Division IA is the most competitive, while Division III is considered to be the least competitive.

Dorm – Short for dormitory, a dorm is an on-campus housing facility. Dorms can provide a range of options from suite-style rooms to more communal options that include shared bathrooms. Most first-year students live in dorms. Some upperclassmen who wish to stay on campus also choose this option.

Early Action – A way to apply to a school and get an early acceptance response without a binding commitment. This is a system that is becoming less and less available.

Early Decision – An option that students should use only if they are positive that a place is their dream school. If a student applies to a school using the early decision option and is admitted, they are required and bound to attend that university. Admission rates are usually higher with early decision students because the school knows that a student is making them their first choice.

Ecstasy – An illegal drug. Also known as "E" or "X," ecstasy looks like a pill and most resembles an aspirin. Considered a party drug, ecstasy is very dangerous and can be deadly.

Ethernet – An extremely fast internet connection that is usually available in most university-owned residence halls. To use an Ethernet connection properly, a student will need a network card and cable for their computer.

Fake ID – A counterfeit identification card that contains false information. Most commonly, students get fake IDs and change their birthdates so that they appear to be older than 21 (of legal drinking age). Even though it is illegal, many college students have fake IDs in hopes of purchasing alcohol or getting into bars.

Frosh – Slang for "freshmen."

Hazing – Initiation rituals that must be completed for membership into some fraternities or sororities. Numerous universities have outlawed hazing due to its degrading or dangerous requirements.

Sports (IMs) – A popular, and usually free, student activity where students create teams and compete against other groups for fun. These sports vary in competitiveness and can include a range of activities—everything from billiards to water polo. IM sports are a great way to meet people with similar interests.

Keg – Officially called a half barrel, a keg contains roughly 200 12-ounce servings of beer and is often found at college parties.

LSD – An illegal drug. Also known as acid, this hallucinogenic drug most commonly resembles a tab of paper.

Marijuana – An illegal drug. Also known as weed or pot; besides alcohol, marijuana is one of the most commonly-found drugs on campuses across the country.

Major –The focal point of a student's college studies; a specific topic that is studied for a degree. Examples of majors include physics, English, history, computer science, economics, business, and music. Many students decide on a specific major before arriving on campus, while others are simply "undecided" and figure it out later. Those who are extremely interested in two areas can also choose to double major.

Meal Block – The equivalent of one meal. Students on a "meal plan" usually receive a fixed number of meals per week.

Each meal, or "block," can be redeemed at the school's dining facilities in place of cash. More often than not, if a student fails to use their weekly allotment of meal blocks, they will be forfeited.

Minor – An additional focal point in a student's education. Often serving as a compliment or addition to a student's main area of focus, a minor has fewer requirements and prerequisites to fulfill than a major. Minors are not required for graduation from most schools; however some students who want to further explore many different interests choose to have both a major and a minor.

Mushrooms – An illegal drug. Also known as "shrooms," this drug looks like regular mushrooms but are extremely hallucinogenic.

Off-Campus Housing – Housing from a particular landlord or rental group that is not affiliated with the university. Depending on the college, off-campus housing can range from extremely popular to non-existent. Those students who choose to live off campus are typically given more freedom, but they also have to deal with things such as possible subletting scenarios, furniture, and bills. In addition to these factors, rental prices and distance often affect a student's decision to move off campus.

Office Hours – Time that teachers set aside for students who have questions about the coursework. Office hours are a good place for students to go over any problems and to show interest in the subject material.

Pledging – The time after a student has gone through rush, received a bid, and has chosen a particular fraternity or sorority they would like to join. Pledging usually lasts anywhere from one to two semesters. Once the pledging period is complete and a particular student has done everything that is required to become a member, they are considered a brother or sister. If a fraternity or a sorority would decide to "haze" a group of students, these initiation rituals would take place during the pledging period.

Private Institution – A school that does not use taxpayers dollars to help subsidize education costs. Private schools typically cost more than public schools and are usually smaller.

Prof – Slang for "professor."

Public Institution – A school that uses taxpayers dollars to help subsidize education costs. Public schools are often a good value for in-state residents and tend to be larger than most private colleges.

Quarter System (sometimes referred to as the Trimester System) – A type of academic calendar system. In this setup, students take classes for three academic periods. The first quarter usually starts in late September or early October and concludes right before Christmas. The second quarter usually starts around early to mid–January and finishes up around March or April. The last quarter, or "third quarter," usually starts in late March or early April and finishes up in late May or Mid-June. The fourth quarter is summer. The major difference between the quarter system and semester system is that students take more courses but with less coverage.

RA (Resident Assistant) – A student leader who is assigned to a particular floor in a dormitory in order to help to the other students who live there. A RA's duties include ensuring student safety and providing guidance or assistance wherever possible.

Recitation – An extension of a specific course; a "review" session of sorts. Because some classes are so large, recitations offer a setting with fewer students where students can ask questions and get help from professors or TAs in a more personalized environment. As a result, it is common for most large lecture classes to be supplemented with recitations.

Rolling Admissions – A form of admissions. Most commonly found at public institutions, schools with this type of policy continue to accept students throughout the year until their class sizes are met. For example, some schools begin accepting students as early as December and will continue to do so until April or May.

Room and Board – This is typically the combined cost of a university-owned room and a meal plan.

Room Draw/Housing Lottery – A common way to pick on-campus room assignments for the following year. If a student decides to remain in university-owned housing, they are assigned a unique number that, along with seniority, is used to choose their new rooms for the next year.

Rush – The period in which students can meet the brothers and sisters of a particular chapter and find out if a given fraternity or sorority is right for them. Rushing a fraternity or a sorority is not a requirement at any school. The goal of rush is to give students who are serious about pledging a feel for what to expect.

Semester System – The most common type of academic calendar system at college campuses. This setup typically includes two semesters in a given school year. The "fall" semester starts around the end of August or early September and finishes right before winter vacation. The "spring" semester usually starts in mid-January and ends around late April or May.

Student Center/Rec Center/Student Union – A common area on campus that often contains study areas, recreation facilities, and eateries. This building is often a good place to meet up with fellow students and is most commonly used as a hangout. Depending on the school, the student center can have a huge role or a non-existent role in campus life.

Student ID – A university-issued photo ID that serves as a student's key to many different functions within an institution. Some schools require students to show these cards in order to get into dorms, libraries, cafeterias, and other facilities. In addition to storing meal plan information, in some cases, a student ID can actually work as a debit card and allow students to purchase things from bookstores or local shops.

Suite – A type of dorm room. Unlike other places that have communal bathrooms that are shared by the entire floor, a suite has a private bathroom. Suite-style dorm rooms can house anywhere from two to ten students.

TA (Teacher's Assistant) – An undergraduate or grad student who helps in some manner with a specific course. In some cases, a TA will teach a class, assist a professor, grade assignments, or conduct office hours.

Undergraduate – A student who is in the process of studying for their Bachelor (college) degree.

ABOUT THE AUTHORS:

It's been a very valuable experience compiling this information about RISD. As a senior, looking back has given me perspective, and a newfound appreciation for what I have gone through, and what I will be taking away with me. RISD has taught me that you can support yourself doing something that you love, and although parts of our society may not feel that art is important, I have found that it touches people in ways far more profound than can be simply expressed. The students and graduates of RISD are the eyes and hands of America; we keep the rest of the country, and the world, seeing beauty. It is our job to observe and display that beauty in every way we can, and that job is important.

I would like to thank the Textiles and English departments for supporting me and teaching me so much, the students who took time out of their busy, busy lives to tell me about themselves, and the people at College Prowler for giving prospective students a chance to better understand what they are getting themselves into.

Brooke Ackerley is a Textile Design major, an English Concentrator (emphasis on poetry), and Co-Founder and Editor of RISD's literary magazine Blackletter.

Notes

Notes

....

....

....

....

....

....

....

....

....

....

....

....

....

....

Notes

....

....

....

....

....

....

....

....

....

....

....

....

....

Notes

....

....

....

....

....

....

....

....

....

....

....

....

....

Notes

Notes

Notes

....

....

....

....

....

....

....

....

....

....

....

....

....

Notes

Notes

....

....

....

....

....

....

....

....

....

....

....

....

....

Notes

....

....

....

....

....

....

....

....

....

....

....

....

....

Notes

Notes

....

....

....

....

....

....

....

....

....

....

....

....

....

Notes

....

....

....

....

....

....

....

....

....

....

....

....

....

Notes

....

....

....

....

....

....

....

....

....

....

....

....

....

Notes

....

....

....

....

....

....

....

....

....

....

....

....

Notes

··

··

··

··

··

··

··

··

··

··

··

··

··

Notes

....

....

....

....

....

....

....

....

....

....

....

....

....

Notes

Notes

....

....

....

....

....

....

....

....

....

....

....

....

....

Need More Help?

Do you have more questions about this school? Can't find a certain statistic? College Prowler is here to help. We are the best source of college information on the planet. We have a network of thousands of students who can get the latest information on any school to you ASAP. E-mail us at *info@collegeprowler.com* with your college-related questions. It's like having an older sibling show you the ropes!

Email Us Your College-Related Questions!

Check out **www.collegeprowler.com** for more details.
1.800.290.2682

Notes

Tell Us What Life Is Really Like At Your School!

Have you ever wanted to let people know what your school is really like? Now's your chance to help millions of high school students choose the right school.

Let your voice be heard and win cash and prizes!

Check out **www.collegeprowler.com** for more info!

Notes

....

....

....

....

....

....

....

....

....

....

....

....

....

Do You Have What It Takes To Get Admitted?

The College Prowler Road to College Counseling Program is here. An admissions officer will review your candidacy at the school of your choice and create a 12+ page personal admission plan. We rate your credentials with the same criteria used by school admissions committees. We assess your strengths and weaknesses and create a plan of action that makes a difference.

Check out **www.collegeprowler.com** or call 1.800.290.2682 for complete details.

Notes

....

....

....

....

....

....

....

....

....

....

....

....

Pros and Cons

Still can't figure out if this is the right school for you?
You've already read through this in-depth guide; why not
list the pros and cons? It will really help with narrowing down
your decision and determining whether or not
this school is right for you.

Pros	Cons

Notes

....

....

....

....

....

....

....

....

....

....

....

....

....

Notes

Notes

....

....

....

....

....

....

....

....

....

....

....

....

....

Notes

Notes

....

....

....

....

....

....

....

....

....

....

....

....

....

Write For Us!
Get Published! Voice Your Opinion.

Writing a College Prowler guidebook is both fun and rewarding; our open-ended format allows your own creativity free reign. Our writers have been featured in national newspapers and have seen their names in bookstores across the country. Now is your chance to break into the publishing industry with one of the country's fastest-growing publishers!

Apply now at **www.collegeprowler.com**

Contact *editor@collegeprowler.com* or call 1.800.290.2682 for more details.

Notes

....

....

....

....

....

....

....

....

....

....

....

....

....

Notes

Notes

···

···

···

···

···

···

···

···

···

···

···

···

···

Notes

....
....
....
....
....
....
....
....
....
....
....
....
....

Notes

....

....

....

....

....

....

....

....

....

....

....

....

....

Notes

Notes

....

....

....

....

....

....

....

....

....

....

....

....

....

Notes

Notes

....

....

....

....

....

....

....

....

....

....

....

....

....

Notes

Notes

SEARCHING FOR CLAIRE (SPECIAL FORCES: OPERATION ALPHA

MOUNTAIN RESCUE
BOOK THREE

JULIA BRIGHT

Dear Readers,

Welcome to the Special Forces: Operation Alpha Fan-Fiction world!

If you are new to this amazing world, in a nutshell the author wrote a story using one or more of my characters in it. Sometimes that character has a major role in the story, and other times they are only mentioned briefly. This is perfectly legal and allowable because they are going through Aces Press to publish the story.

This book is entirely the work of the author who wrote it. While I might have assisted with brainstorming and other ideas about which of my characters to use, I didn't have any part in the process or writing or editing the story.

I'm proud and excited that so many authors loved my characters enough that they wanted to write them into their own story. Thank you for supporting them, and me!

READ ON!
Xoxo
Susan Stoker

CHAPTER ONE

Claire Draven breathed in the thick, humid air of the forest, savoring the earthy scent as she wandered down the path, taking in the rainbow of flowers sprinkled here and there. The place was beautiful, quiet, and not at all like Baltimore, where she lived with her mom and dad.

At the first hint of light outside her window this morning, she'd rolled out of bed, determined to enjoy the area. And she was enjoying this walk around the small lake near the house she and her family had rented. She pushed away the pressures threatening to overtake her thoughts and concentrated on the birds flying overhead. That was true freedom. But then again, birds didn't get the pleasure of a good pedicure or snuggling deep under the blankets and reading until noon on Sunday.

Maybe if she lived in a town like Fallport, the

weight on her shoulders would be reduced. She sighed, wishing some parts of her life were different. At twenty-two, she hadn't thought she would still be working for her dad, but he paid well, and she enjoyed her work for the most part.

If she'd continued at the university and left the family business, she would probably be in an even bigger city than Baltimore, working hard just to afford an apartment the size of a closet. But she'd listened to her parents, and they'd convinced her to come home and work for the family. They all agreed it had been the right decision.

She shrugged, pushing away the desire to leave her family's business and move out on her own. Work, no matter who it was for, would be stressful. Yes, her parents expected her to do a lot, maybe more than a non-family member would have to do, but she was their daughter, and she wanted to make them proud.

As she made the turn at the far end of the lake, she spied a brown rabbit near a bush. The rabbit paused and watched her for a moment before taking off into the underbrush. The sun had turned the sky a soft pink color, and she caught glimpses of oranges and purples in the clouds at the horizon between the trees. She wished she was above the tree line and could see the magnificence of colors.

Another animal made a sound, and her attention turned to the forest. The thick underbrush in this area hid secrets she wanted to discover...unless the secret was a snake or bear. Those she could do without.

Her family liked to sleep in on vacation. She didn't blame them, but they also liked to stay up late and party. This trip was different from their usual beach or Vegas holidays. She'd picked the place, and though they'd grumbled a bit, they seemed happy to be out here in the wild, well, nearly wild. Tonight, they would camp under the stars. Her parents weren't keen on it, but they'd agreed.

Claire had been waiting her whole life to camp like this. She wanted to be out where she could see the sparkling diamond-like stars splashed against the velvety black sky without city lights making it impossible to view them. She appreciated lights on dark streets when she was out at night, but she longed to see stars above.

They would pick up their tent packs—she checked her watch—in seven hours. An excited giggle escaped her lips. It was really happening.

She still had a lot to do, like make sure everyone had what they needed. They still had the house for the rest of the week, so they were leaving their suitcases in place, but she'd instructed each member of her family to pack what they would need on this part of the trip in a backpack.

Once everyone was up, the chaos of the cabin would take over, and she would oversee their preparations, managing everyone, though she was the youngest of the kids. For some reason, she was the most responsible when it came to getting places on time. They depended on her for almost everything, and she guessed she liked it that way. She knew what everyone needed, like when they had doctor appointments, where they were supposed to be, and when they should leave. Sometimes, she wished she didn't have to direct them all, but responsibility was part of being a family.

The sky had shifted from purple to orange and pink and settled on blue as she took the final turn to head back to the cabin. Light glimmered on the placid lake, and a wistful feeling fluttered through her. If she lived here year-round, she would never get tired of the raw beauty.

The big city exhausted her, and she wanted peace and quiet. Baltimore had too many people, too much noise, and way too much crime. She longed for daily walks like this, the tranquility, the beauty, the happiness she felt just being in nature.

Claire hesitated, not wanting to return to the house just yet. She should go back and get everything ready, but why did she always have to be the responsible one? A sliver of guilt twisted through her, but she pushed it away. Her family would be fine if she did something, just one little thing, for herself.

She spied a path that led to the quaint downtown area of Fallport. The house they'd rented was close to the downtown area, something she'd done to appease her parents. Though this downtown wasn't at all what her mother had been expecting. There wasn't a long row of shops she could while her hours away in, trying on dress after dress.

Claire rolled her eyes. Her mother had been very unhappy when they'd first arrived, but then they'd started drinking. She closed her eyes and blew out a breath, trying not to focus on the negatives. This vacation was good. They were enjoying themselves. So what if this wasn't like Vegas? That was the point.

The scent of bacon wafted over her, and her stomach rumbled. Her eyes popped open, and she glanced back to the house where her family slept. It was still early, and none of her family would be awake. They wouldn't miss her. She thought about returning to the cabin to take care of some task she was sure no one else would do, but the bacon smelled too good. She couldn't think of any good reason not to find where that delicious scent was coming from.

Her mind made up, she turned away from the house and headed toward town. She smiled to herself, happy to be here. She loved being in nature. The air was fresher, and the sun shone brighter. Even the flowers looked better here.

The quaint town of Fallport was more than she'd expected. This was the type of place holiday movies were written about. It wasn't winter, or even fall, but she could imagine how beautiful this place would be with a little dusting of snow, carolers singing happy songs, people with rosy cheeks as they walked down the main street hand in hand, chestnuts roasting—did people roast chestnuts anymore? No question, she would have to make another trip here once the weather turned cold, maybe even in December when the holiday decorations were out.

Claire spotted a diner and drew in a deep breath, almost passing out from the delicious scent. She couldn't help but be drawn to the place. "Sunny Side Up," she said to herself as she approached the building. She felt like everything had come up sunny today.

She took a moment to study the inside of the diner as she approached. The place looked packed. Maybe she could find a seat at the counter if there were no open tables. When she opened the door, the scent of bacon and hash browns hit and almost brought her to her knees.

She smiled and stepped in, excitement pumping through her. But the thrill faded as she realized every table had someone at it and the counter stools were all taken. She would have to find another place to eat. But there was no way she could walk away from here. The scent was too good.

Her gaze landed on a man with broad shoulders, wavy dark hair, and a five o'clock shadow, though it was six in the morning. His nose looked like it had been broken before and bent to the left. His head lifted, and his gaze connected with hers, catching and holding for a long moment. He narrowed his eyes and then glanced around before landing back on her.

Butterflies swarmed in her stomach, and her knees went weak. It had been ages since she'd felt anything like this. She hadn't given up dating, but when did she have time for anyone other than work and family? She gripped her hands in front of her body, trying not to squirm under his gaze. If only she could look away, but the intensity held her captive.

When he lifted his hand and waved her over, heat filled her. It would be dangerous to sit with him. Not that she had anything to hide other than her overactive libido that had seemed to come alive at the sight of him. Maybe she should leave. But what harm could come from eating at his table? It wasn't like this was a date, though her body was on fire just from holding his gaze.

CHAPTER TWO

"Might as well sit with Eric, though he's not a big talker." A tall, skinny woman with a huge smile approached, handed her a menu, and directed her toward the table where the man with incredible sex appeal sat.

Her face had to be red based on the heat rising up her neck. Was everyone staring? She glanced around and noticed that most people were eating, but there were a few people looking at her as she hesitantly stepped over to his table.

He wore jeans and a navy-blue shirt with the sleeves rolled up to his elbows. His forearms were much bigger than hers, and his biceps pulled at the material like they needed to escape. Just the thought of him taking off his shirt brought more heat. She pushed the thoughts away as she focused on his shoulders.

Sweet baby Jesus, the closer she got, the more muscular his arms and shoulders appeared.

"T-thank you for letting me sit here," she said as she slid into the seat, picking up the scent of coffee and maybe sandalwood coming off him.

His lips spread into a wide smile, and he nodded. He kept his gaze on her face, not raking over her body like so many men who came to her father's business did. They made her feel cheap and dirty, but this man seemed different. Heck, he could probably crush all those men she had to deal with on a daily basis.

"I'm Claire, and wow, this place is packed. Though I'm not surprised because it smells so good," she said once she settled.

The man chuckled, and the sound shot all the way to her core. "It does smell good. My name's Eric." His low voice rumbled between them. She had to cross her legs to stop the feeling from taking over.

She didn't want to act like a fool, so she focused on breathing slowly and forcing a calm she certainly didn't feel. "It's really nice for you to let me sit here. Where I live, I'd be out of luck."

He chuckled, the sound once again shooting straight through her. She met his eyes and almost gasped at the beautiful brown color that had much more depth than she'd ever seen before.

"You must be here on vacation?"

Claire nodded. "Yeah, we—my parents and brothers—

rented a house near here. We're headed out camping for a few nights, and then we'll be back at the end of the week. I guess we've been in town for two days so far. We needed a break. Work has been tough, and I decided to force my parents to take a vacation." She slapped her hand over her mouth. After a second, she uncovered her mouth and rolled her eyes. "Sorry, I'm rambling. That waitress said you don't talk much, and obviously, I talk way too much."

"I didn't notice," he said with a soft laugh. "Talking is okay. I just don't say much unless I have something to say."

She lifted one shoulder. "Makes sense—not saying something unless you have something to say. I just think I have a lot to say most days. But thank you for letting me sit with you." She reached across the table, holding out her hand so she could shake his.

Eric's lips tipped up on one side as he reached for her hand. The second their skin touched, she felt a spark fly between them. He must have felt something, too, because his eyes went wide, and his lips parted. She expected him to immediately drop her hand. Instead, he squeezed once. His touch felt warm and inviting, and she wanted to know more about him and find out if his touch in other places would make her feel as good.

Then the waitress bumped their table with her hip. Embarrassment twisted through Claire. She pulled back her hand, dropping it to her lap.

The woman's lips quirked up as she gestured at the menu. "Do you want something? Coffee? Tea?"

"Coffee, never tea," Claire said.

"Sure thing, hun. I'm Lisa, by the way. I'm new here, only in town for the summer season, but I'll take good care of you two."

"I'll have some more coffee," Eric said.

"Sure. Do you all want the breakfast special?" Lisa asked.

Claire looked at the menu, seeing the special had too much food for her to eat. "I'll have two eggs scrambled, bacon, and hash browns."

"I'll have the special," Eric said.

"Coming right up," Lisa said.

Lisa took off, and Eric sat back, meeting her gaze. "I never understood the appeal of hot tea. Iced tea, I can drink all day long."

Claire smiled and nodded. "I agree, though I don't like sweet tea."

"Same," Eric said.

Get up and run whispered through her mind, but she also wanted to know more about this man. Why? She would never see him again, but for some reason, she needed the information. "Do you live here?"

"Sure do. I have for the last five years. When I got out of the Marines, I moved here."

Her gaze flicked to his incredibly thick forearms. "Oh, nice. So what do you do here in Fallport?"

"I like working with wood," Eric said. "Right now, I

work for a builder part-time, but I also make furniture."

The thick muscles made sense. He'd earned them with real work. "Wow, that's impressive. You make furniture. I'd love to see it."

"He makes nice furniture," Lisa said as she poured them coffee. "He has some over at the shop close to downtown. It's worth the stop for a look-see."

"Thanks, Lisa." Eric's lips tipped up on one side.

"No problem, hun." Lisa walked away and poured coffee for another table.

Eric tapped the table between them. "So what about you?"

She shrugged. "For now, I'm the bookkeeper for my father's company. I wanted to go to college for music, but my dad made me come home after the first semester. I'm good at math, but I don't like it. But that's all I do all day. It's not very exciting, really." Embarrassment twisted through her. She hadn't acknowledged to anyone that her parents made her come home, but that's what it had felt like deep inside. Why was she telling this guy the unadulterated truth?

"Do you think you'll go back to college?"

"I don't know," Claire said. "Maybe."

Lisa came past and poured them more coffee before she breezed off to take another order.

Eric took a sip of coffee and lifted his eyebrows. "Where do you live?"

Claire's lips twitched up. "Outside of Baltimore. I

know I don't have an accent, but that's because we lived in Oklahoma for the first six years of my life, then we moved to California. We've only been in Baltimore for the last eight years."

Eric chuckled. "You do have an accent, but it's not thick. I can hear a bit of a southern twang on some words and a bit of the Baltimore thing."

"The Baltimore thing? Oh God, I'm a hodgepodge of accents."

"It's not too bad, but you definitely have dropped more than a few letters while speaking."

She rolled her eyes, then chuckled. "And here I thought I was doing good."

He shrugged, then drank more coffee. She liked the way his eyes crinkled when he laughed or smiled. It was odd how she'd come here for vacation and finally met a man who really interested her.

"What type of music do you like best?" Eric asked.

She shrugged. "Honestly, I like American folk music. Not necessarily country, more like bluegrass. I also enjoy calypso and the music generated by black artists. I've studied some of the earliest music recorded by black performers. The songs are amazing. Especially when you get into what was produced in New Orleans. Which is a style all on its own. I guess I just like the older, folksy music."

"Wow, that's impressive. I guess I haven't given music much thought. I'm more the kind of person that just listens to whatever is on."

Lisa dropped off their plates, and they dug in. The first bite of bacon on Claire's tongue brought forth a moan. She closed her eyes and savored the delicious flavor. She thought the food was some of the best she'd ever eaten.

"It's good food," Eric said when he caught her eye.

She nodded appreciatively. "So good."

A couple stopped by and said hello to Eric, and a few more people waved at him as they walked past. He commented about each person, telling her some interesting facts about them but never anything mean. His easy charm captivated her. He seemed like a very nice person.

At home, her father never had anything nice to say about anyone. It bugged her, but she'd always passed it off.

Doing her father's books wasn't a good fit for her. She worked for him because he asked her to. Sometimes he told her to do things with the numbers that she didn't think was right, but it was his company, and what choice did she have? He knew how to do the books and what everyone expected. Last month, he'd asked her to omit some payments to him. She'd argued at first that she had to include them, but after he explained that those payments were for a side business that she knew nothing about, she deleted them from the official log. It felt wrong, but what choice did she have?

They were almost done with their meal when she got a text from her brother.

"Everything okay?" Eric asked.

"Ugh, yes. My brother wants me to make him breakfast. I swear, sometimes I wonder if I'm just a servant. They act like they can't do anything on their own."

Guilt filled her as the words drifted over the table. She was complaining, which was wrong. They'd done so much for her. She started typing her reply, wishing she'd taken a vacation alone instead of dragging her family along.

"I'm telling him he can make his own breakfast. He knows how to make food."

After she sent the text, she glanced up, noticing the smirk on Eric's face.

"What? Am I being too mean?" She bit her lower lip as worry exploded through her.

He shook his head. "How old are your brothers?"

"Older than me. I'm twenty-one, so Blaine is twenty-three, and Mike is twenty-four."

Eric's lips turned into a deep frown, and she worried that he thought she was being a jerk to her brothers. Her parents would have forced her to go make them breakfast. That's how it was at home. She did everything for everyone. Sometimes, she worried that she was just being used.

"Oh, heck no. You are not being mean at all. By the time I was twenty, I was cooking and cleaning for myself unless I ate on base. They can make their own meals."

She appreciated his words. He was right. Her brothers were old enough to cook for themselves. Why did she always have to do everything for everyone?

Her lips tipped up as good feelings spread. She wished they were actually friends. Work kept her very busy, so she didn't have many friends to go out with. "I want to see your furniture, but I fear I have to go back to the house and fix their food." Had she said too much? Surely this man didn't need or want her friendship.

He shrugged. "We could exchange numbers."

Claire felt like she'd fallen down a hole and entered a completely different realm, where magical things happened. No hot guys ever wanted to give her their number, and here was this incredibly sexy man who sent sparks flying through her, offering up his personal number.

She clutched her hands in her lap to keep from doing something silly, like fluttering them or clapping excitedly. "Sure. I'd love that." She clenched her hands into fists, pushing away the glee running through her, then grabbed her phone, opened the contacts, and held it out to him. "Here you go. Just put in your name and number."

He nodded and typed in his information before handing it back to her. She automatically texted him with her full name.

"There, now you have my name and number. I look forward to hearing from you."

Claire hadn't brought her purse, but had forty dollars stuffed in her pocket.

She met Eric's gaze and flashed a smile. "Do you think this is over twenty?"

He shook his head. "I doubt yours is even ten."

"Well, I guess dropping a twenty is good, then. And thank you for letting me sit here. I really enjoyed talking to you." She stood and was about to move away when she got a wild idea. Instead of walking out the door, she moved closer to Eric and leaned in, kissing his cheek. Heat filled her. She couldn't believe she'd been so bold.

She dashed for the door, but turned back to glance at him one more time. His eyes held hers for a long second before someone stepped between them, breaking his eye contact.

She pushed out the front door and took off in the wrong direction. But she couldn't rush back past the diner, so she took the long way, looping the block before heading back to the house they were renting.

Maybe he would forget her, and she'd never hear from him, but she would never forget him. He was handsome, kind, and hella sexy. The chance of ever seeing him again was extremely low. She just hoped he wasn't mad that she'd kissed his cheek. She didn't know what had come over her, but she'd felt the need to be close to this man, even if only for a few seconds.

CHAPTER THREE

Eric couldn't help but smile as he walked away from the diner. He hopped into his truck and flipped on the radio, listening to the country music station as he drove out to the house they were currently building. As the music changed from one song to the next, he wondered if Claire would like this. She'd said folksy music and not necessarily country. He didn't know if there was a station like that for the area. Honestly, he'd never really even looked.

He pulled onto Green Mountain Run Road, driving with caution because of the early morning deer crossings. This road was away from town and had a dead-end at a mostly unused trailhead. This was where he would spend his day working. The drive was pleasant, with no deer darting out. He groaned loudly as the monstrosity came into view. The home was too large for Fallport, but the guy wanted a big house even though nothing else in the area was this huge. If the man ever tried to sell this monstrosity, getting rid of it would take a long time. The people in this area weren't ostentatious. Instead, they were more salt of the earth types. Some of them had money, but most were humble people with solid jobs that they worked hard at. He didn't know why this person wanted such a huge home here.

Eric wasn't the first on the lot, but he wasn't the last one, either. He grabbed his tools and started to work. He should finish a few tasks today, and maybe he could stay home and work on a project he wanted to complete tomorrow.

Eric focused on the tasks at hand and was minding his own business when the first comment was made.

"So, who was that girl you were all doe-eyed with this morning at Sunny Side Up?" Matt asked.

He finished with the hammer and glanced up, then shrugged. "Just someone who needed a place to sit."

Ben chuckled. "A place to sit. You mean on your face, right?" Ben cackled like a hen after he spoke.

Heat filled Eric at the thought, and he shook his head. "Jesus, guys, give it a break. We ate breakfast while sitting at the same table. That was it."

"But you gave her your number. You want her to sit on your face," another guy called out from across the expanse.

Heat rose up his neck, and he had little doubt that his cheeks were red. These guys gave each other hell for dating women in town or neighboring towns. Hitting on a vacationer would draw heat from them. He'd known that when talking to Claire, but he hadn't cared. She made him feel things he hadn't felt in ages. He knew getting this way over someone here on vacation was stupid, but he couldn't help his reaction to the woman.

The second she stepped into the diner, it was like a light had shown on her. Almost like someone from above was telling him she was the one. Not that he'd ever thought there was one perfect woman for him, but Claire might just be that person.

"She's a nice woman," Eric said.

"So when's the wedding?" Matt's cackling laughter filled the area.

Eric rolled his eyes, then finished with the section he was working on before heading to another part of the house to finish some work. His thoughts stayed on Claire as he worked in the bathroom.

She was cute and nice, someone he would be interested in getting to know. He wished she lived closer. He shouldn't get too caught up with thoughts of her because he would probably never see her again, which was just as well. He wasn't really looking to date anyone.

At lunch, his phone pinged, and he saw a text from Claire asking which souvenir she should buy. One was a T-shirt, the other a wooden wind chime he'd made. He didn't make many chimes, but he used the leftover wood from projects and carved it into shapes and pipes when he had time. Some of the pieces were difficult based on the design, but he enjoyed the challenge.

ERIC: The wind chime. I made it.

Claire: Are you kidding me? This is beautiful. I'm so buying it.

ERIC SMILED TO HIMSELF, thankful he'd given her his number. He pulled up his photo album of furniture he'd made and sent Claire a shot of the last table he'd made for a client.

CLAIRE: That is amazing. I want to see some of your furniture in person.

Eric: I could arrange that.

Claire: Once we're back in town, I'll text you. Thank you for sharing the photo with me.

ERIC SMILED TO HIMSELF, then tucked his phone away. He still had four more hours on this job, and he had a lot to get accomplished. The work was easy, and his mind drifted to Claire. She was beautiful and young, but not too young. She had a cute mouth, a button nose, and beautiful brown eyes, and her body was nice and curvy. He'd tried not to let his gaze dip and stare at her chest, but he'd seen that she was nicely endowed. The thought of her pressed up against him made him hard, so he pushed those thoughts away.

Claire and her family were going to camp in tents. The local companies usually told campers where to head. The location was relatively safe, and the hike to and from the campsite was short. She was with her family, so it wasn't like she would be out there all alone. He didn't need to worry about her. They wouldn't get lost, and hopefully, they wouldn't encounter any dangerous wildlife. Usually, city dwellers were loud and chased away bears and bobcats long before they would have seen them.

His phone pinged, and he glanced down at the screen. He saw it was Claire, and he put his tools down and decided to take his afternoon break.

CLAIRE: How do you feel about being places on time?

HE SCRATCHED HIS JAW, wondering if this was a trick question. Maybe it was best he told her upfront how he felt about it instead of hiding his thoughts on tardiness.

ERIC: I think being on time is important.

Claire: Thank goodness. My family is two hours

23

late leaving the house. We have to be at the trailhead in five minutes. I'm about to lose my mind.

Eric: I like being on time. Scratch that. Early. I don't like being late for stuff.

Claire: Same. They are finally ready to move. I'll chat with you once we make it back to civilization.

HE WISHED she wasn't headed out to a no cell phone reception area, but maybe a day or so of no communication would allow him to wrap his head around how he felt about her. She made him feel again. It had been a while since he'd dated. Four years, to be exact. He hadn't found anyone after Shea, and honestly, he hadn't been looking.

After work, he stopped by On The Rocks to check in with the guys. Cohen, Talon, and Brock were there discussing plans for the coming months. They were planning on doing another training session for locals on how to make it back to town safely. Most locals were well-seasoned in hiking, but they could always use a refresher.

A couple of the guys got up to use the restroom and grab another beer. Eric pulled out his phone and checked it, though he knew Claire wouldn't have been able to text.

"Hey, why are you checking your phone?" Cohen asked as he slid onto the stool.

Eric shrugged and then rolled his eyes. "I'm being ridiculous."

"Is it that woman you were eating breakfast with?" Talon asked.

Eric gasped. "Has everyone heard about me eating with Claire?"

Brock chuckled. "I'm surprised people haven't started planning your wedding."

Eric shook his head. "Some guys at work asked me about that today."

"What did you tell them?" Talon asked.

"Duh, I'm not marrying someone I just met. But she is cute as heck," Eric said.

"Cute is good," Talon said.

"So," Cohen dragged out the word as he leaned in. "Where is she from? How old is she? Give us some details so we don't have to go searching for the town gossips."

Eric narrowed his gaze. "I'm not gossiping about her."

Cohen shrugged. "I'll hear about it tomorrow anyway when I go into the coffee shop."

Brock and Talon snorted. Everyone knew who the gossips were and how to avoid them. But they did drop some interesting information at times. He just tried to avoid them and never let them know his business.

That evening as he sat on his back porch, whittling away at a piece of wood, he thought about Claire. The wood chunk in his hands started to take shape. An hour later, he realized he was carving a butterfly for Claire. Maybe he was getting too wrapped up in thoughts about her, but he couldn't ignore the pull he felt while in her presence. There was something between them, and he hoped he had a chance to explore the feelings.

CHAPTER FOUR

Having such a late start didn't help at all. The sun was close to setting, and they couldn't get the main tent up. They had the smaller tent she planned to sleep in assembled, but they still had her parents' tent and the one her brothers planned to sleep in left to assemble. Claire was ready to tell her family they should go back to town when her brother finally got the pole threaded through the proper way, and the tent stood on its own. Now her parents had a place to sleep.

"Thank goodness," her mother stated as she moved to the tent's opening.

"No shoes," Claire called out.

Her mother huffed out a breath and rolled her eyes. "Fine. I just want to lay down and get some rest."

Claire should have done this alone. Maybe she wouldn't have felt comfortable camping alone, but she didn't like how her mom kept complaining about everything. Most of the problems had been caused by her parents and her brothers. They'd delayed getting out here, not wanting to spray for bugs, complained about the lack of cellular service, and then complained when Claire demanded they pick up the trash they'd thrown on the ground after eating chips.

Frustration slid through her. Being angry with her family wouldn't help. They didn't like it when she complained about anything. If she brought up something she was dissatisfied with, they would turn it around and make sure she felt guilty for complaining.

They needed to build a fire and set up the rest of the tents. Her father had tried gathering wood, but he'd only brought back sopping wet logs, some of which were covered in mud. It was almost like he was trying to do things wrong.

"We need dry wood, Dad."

Her dad shrugged. "There isn't any."

"We'll have to look for it," she said.

Her dad glanced around and shook his head as he stared at the tree line. "It's dark in there."

"It's a forest, and the sun is setting," she said. "We need a fire."

"Frank, just go get the wood!" her mother yelled, causing birds to squawk and take off from their perches in trees.

Claire cringed as her father rolled his eyes and waved his hand in acknowledgment. She watched her dad head into the forest.

"Fine," her dad called over his shoulder. "You two don't have to be so mean about it."

Claire blew out a breath as her father stalked away. She wasn't being mean, but even asking the simple questions caused him to strike out. And anytime her mother requested anything, her father got angry. No way would her father bring back anything usable. She would have to look for wood and make sure her brothers got their tent up.

She moved to the other side of the clearing, keeping a watchful eye on Blaine and Mike. They were making progress on their tent. It was a lot like their parents' tent but smaller. It took a while, but she found some wood, not much, but a limb was down, and it wasn't soaked.

The sun had sunk lower and lower in the sky and was almost gone when she made it to the fire pit. She struck a match and was thankful when the leaves she'd gathered caught fire, then started to burn the limbs she'd broken and placed over the leaves.

Her brother Blaine came over and held up a bag. "What are these?"

She turned, and her mouth dropped open. "Didn't you put in the tent stakes?"

Blaine shrugged. "Was I supposed to?"

"Ugh. Help me get them in." They hammered in the last tent stake about ten minutes later. Now the tents were all up, and the fire was going. Her dad had come back and put two logs on the fire, thankfully not extinguishing what she'd built. Thick smoke rose as the log her father put on heated up. Great, at least the fire was still going. It was almost like her father wasn't even trying.

"We did it," her father said as he cracked open a beer. At least they wouldn't have to carry the beer back. That would lighten their load. She'd been worried about how heavy their packs had been, but her father and brothers insisted they needed the beer. They hadn't been going far, just a few miles to the camping area. She wanted to hike for a longer distance but knew there was no way her family could have actually done a real hike.

When they were picking up their tent packs and the two food packs the company provided, she'd been worried that her brothers would insist they camp at a different spot, but the man helping them had said they had to camp at the official location. It had taken her brothers more than a few minutes to accept that the official camping spot would be best. If they'd gone deeper into the woods, they wouldn't have gotten the tents up before dark, and there was a chance they wouldn't have made it at all.

Satisfied, Claire moved away from the circle of light and stared up at the stars. It was beautiful out here. She wanted more of this, but next vacation, she wasn't going to invite her family. Maybe Eric would appreciate camping.

"I'm glad we got the tent up." Her mother's voice

was very close, and Claire jerked back, almost running into her.

"All because of me," Mike said as he slapped his chest.

Claire rolled her eyes and shook off the unease. Sometimes she got this way around her family. She loved them and liked being around them, but sometimes they did things that unsettled her. She couldn't pinpoint it. It was like something creeping along her skin, making the hairs rise. Silly, she knew. They were her family and wouldn't do anything to hurt her.

She smirked at Mike and shook her head. "Please, you were too busy taking photos of yourself."

Blaine came over and leaned in close, his eyes widened, and his lips spread into a wicked grin. "It's so quiet here. It's almost spooky."

Claire fought to suppress a shiver. Again the hairs rose on her arms. "Stop. It's not spooky. It's nice, peaceful."

"I think it's nice," her mother said, her voice drifting off as she stared at the forest around them.

"We got the fire going, so we can eat," her father said.

"I'm ready for food." Her brother beat his chest with his fists, acting like a gorilla.

"Hey, dufus, we're not in Africa," Claire said. She enjoyed how silly they were. There were times at work they seemed way too serious. These good times made quitting her music and moving home worthwhile in some ways. She still longed for what she'd given up by coming home, but it was silly to dwell on it. Her father had been right, and she would have never made anything of herself in music. She didn't have enough talent, and folk music wasn't popular. She would have been penniless, or worse, working for a huge corporation.

Blaine's lips turned down in a frown, and his eyes narrowed. "What does that mean?"

"You were imitating a gorilla. You know, from Africa, not America," she said.

Blaine slapped her on the back of her head as he walked past.

"Hey," she called out as she winced.

"You're here and funny looking. I thought we were in a zoo," Blaine said.

"I have food. Chili and beans. Let's eat," her mom said, cutting off the argument.

Claire pushed away the weirdness, vowing to be better with her brothers. She knew they could get angry sometimes, and keeping the peace was up to her.

She helped serve the food before sitting next to her mom. This was what she wanted. A simple meal around the campfire with the stars shining above. She wished her family could be like this all the time. No one complained, maybe because they were all too tired.

After they finished eating, her mom opened two packages of cookies, passing them around while Claire cleaned the pan their meal had been cooked in. After she finished cleaning, she took a seat on a log near her dad. He started talking about business, and she listened while she nibbled two cookies. Her brothers both had a beer while she stuck to water.

She knew enough about the business to do the books, but she felt like there was a huge part she missed out on. When she listened to her father and brothers talk about the business, it was like there was some context she didn't get, like something under the surface that didn't add up. That wasn't her concern, though, just the books. She needed to take a book-keeping class and make sure she was doing everything right because something felt off. She would eventually take the course and figure it out.

The night air grew cool, but the warmth of the crackling fire kept her comfortable. Contentment and happiness wove through her. She could get used to this. Maybe not sleeping in a tent and not having a kitchen or bathroom, but the peacefulness of this place appealed to her.

Exhaustion started to seep in, and she stood and stretched. "I need sleep."

"Yeah, we all do," her dad said.

Her mother and brothers stood and stretched. This was how she imagined their vacation going, them all getting along, happiness filling them, and life being easy. Contentment bubbled up as she brushed her teeth and prepared for bed. She broke up the logs on the fire and made sure it would die down before she headed into her tent.

The day's anxieties and worries melted as she lay in her sleeping bag, listening to the gentle sounds of the forest. Everything—maybe not everything—had gone right today, or close to right. Sure, her family had been late, but they'd made it here. She'd eaten a good meal by the fire, and no one had really argued. She still didn't understand everything her father and brothers had said about the business, but she would soon. She wanted to be more involved. Maybe after this week, her dad would let her take over another task.

She drifted off to sleep, happy with her life. This place was perfect, and she knew the night would be peaceful.

But she was wrong.

A loud noise sounded close by, and Claire flashed open her eyes, her breathing heavy as she tried to determine if the noise had been real or something she'd imagined in her dream. Darkness surrounded the tent, and she could barely make out her hand in front of her face. It was almost like her eyes were still closed. She grabbed her phone, and though she had no service, she had the flashlight.

She turned it on, positioning it so she could see the zipper. She'd brought her shoes into the tent before sleeping, so she grabbed them and pulled them on. The chill that had settled over the forest during the night barely penetrated the tent, but she felt a waft of cold near the zipper. She grabbed her jacket, wondering if whatever she'd heard was an animal or maybe someone from her family.

A loud snap, like someone stepping on a twig, sounded close by. Worry rushed through her like a freight train. What if it was a bear? She didn't want to be mauled, but she needed to figure out who was outside her tent.

There was another snap, but no heavy breathing other than her own breath filling the tent. Claire drew in a deep breath and held it for a moment before letting go. She needed to calm down. She didn't want to be eaten by a wild animal, but she didn't want her family eaten, either.

She was about to move when the tent's zipper rose, creating an opening. She froze as fear pumped hard.

What was happening?

Claire watched in horror as a man ducked into her tent. The flashlight on her phone bounced off the barrel of a gun. She yelped as he reached for her, pulling her close.

"Get up and outside," the man barked.

Claire almost peed her pants as she scrambled outside. The man pulled her up before he shoved her hard, knocking her to the ground. Her hands slapped the dirt, her palm finding a sharp stick, sending pain up her arm.

Her dad stood in the clearing, fear dripping off him

like water after a storm. Why were these men here? What did they want?

"Move, now. And don't try anything funny. We'll kill you if you do. Got that, Frank?"

At the mention of her father's name, a wave of fear washed over Claire. These men knew who they were. How long had they been following them?

"Move!" the guy yelled.

Everything shook as she made her way over to where her father and brothers stood. She tried to catch her father's gaze, but he wouldn't look at her.

She wanted to ask so many questions. Who were these men? What would they do? A shiver snaked down her spine. Maybe she didn't want to know what these men would do.

The men's faces weren't visible, and they all wore some sort of goggles covering their eyes. They had on long-sleeve shirts and gloves. She had no idea if they had pale skin or dark. Their hair was covered, so she couldn't even get any hints about them based on hair color. They were all taller than she was and spoke English well enough to make her think they weren't from another country. They kind of sounded like some of the punks who lived in Baltimore and hung out at the boxing gyms.

Fear for her dad increased as the men pushed him away from the rest of the family. She wanted to call out and demand they tell her what they were doing.

"You owe us, Frank. And we're going to make sure

you pay up." The man speaking was tall with broad shoulders, and he wore black boots. That was about as detailed as she could get with her description.

"Please don't hurt my family," Frank begged.

The tall man with black boots turned and punched Blaine in the stomach. Claire jerked away, but the man standing behind her grabbed her hair and yanked hard so she was up against his body.

"This one's feisty," the guy holding her hair said. His deep chuckle made her stomach turn.

"I'll make you a deal," Black Boots said.

"Just don't hurt them," Frank had tears in his eyes, and Claire wanted to help him, but she didn't know how.

"We'll keep the feisty one, and you get the money taken care of. Once we get paid, Feisty will come home."

"No!" her mother shrieked.

The man closest to her mother yanked her mom to him, holding her head near his crotch. Her father yelled, but nothing he said or did made them stop. Her mother struggled to get away, but the man punched her. Claire gasped as her mother dropped to the dirt. Mike was there beside her mom, cradling her head.

These men didn't care how much they hurt her family. Claire had no clue what they were talking about. She wished she had a weapon, but against these men, it might not have done any good. They were well-armed and proficient in delivering pain, and she and her family weren't.

"Get us the money you owe us. We got a deal, Frank?" Black Boots asked.

Her father nodded, his gaze straying away from her. Why wouldn't he look at her? The man holding Claire spun her and tossed her over his shoulder, then took off toward the trees. Her heart raced as terror filled her.

She was being taken captive by men her father owed money to. Would she survive? Pain slithered through her with each step taken over the rough ground. Her arms went numb, and her head pounded. The guy didn't put her down for a long time. By the time her feet landed on the ground, the sun was up.

"Put these on," Black Boots said, tossing cuffs at her. They landed in front of her feet. "And keep up. We'll drag you if we have to."

CHAPTER FIVE

Eric had maybe ten more minutes of work left on the porch rail Chief Hill had called him about. The rail had fallen over when his grandkids had been in town. Luckily no one had been injured.

He was about to hammer in a nail when a van screeched to a halt at the curb. Eric set his hammer down as the van doors flew open, and four people spilled out. They didn't shut the doors or seem to care that other stuff, like packs and bags, were falling out of the van.

For a moment, he feared for Chief Hill. Then a police car pulled into the driveway, and the door beside Eric flew open. His heart sped up, and he thought about picking up his hammer again to help defend the police chief.

Eric studied the family, trying to make out what was going on. The father, the leader of the pack, had a look on his face that Eric could easily recognize as grief and something else. The mother had her hands clasped together in front of her, and tears ran down her face. The boys, not children but not older than thirty, looked equal parts sad and resigned. Their faces bore the same expression of despair that their parents wore.

Chief Hill paused, apprehension rolling off him in waves. This didn't seem like a friendly visit.

"Something wrong?" Eric asked as he moved toward the steps, blocking the path to the chief.

The father narrowed his gaze, and his frown deepened. "We're here to see the chief," he said. His voice broke, and he might have even shed a tear.

Eric glanced back at Hill, questioning what he should do. Hill nodded, so Eric stepped aside. He watched the family intently, making sure they weren't carrying weapons. If any of them pulled a gun, he would have to do something. Maybe dive for his hammer and throw it. But that might not do any good.

Tension filled the air as the man from the van stepped closer, and his face crumbled. Something was terribly wrong. The father began to speak to the police chief, grief making his voice break.

"I'm Mr. Draven. We've come because our daughter —" Sobs wracked the man, and he couldn't finish his sentence.

One of the boys stepped closer. "Our sister, Claire, has been taken hostage."

"What?" Chief Hill asked.

"We were camping," the other brother said.

A chill raced through Eric, and he had to fight the urge to gasp. What were the odds this was the same Claire he'd eaten breakfast with? Panic raced through him. He didn't want to imagine that woman being in danger. They hadn't known each other for more than an hour, and they'd texted a few times, but the connection he felt for Claire had been real. Fear rose, making it difficult to breathe.

Eric had tuned out their words but tuned back in as Hill said something. "Do you know where they are?"

The man shook his head, and a sob escaped from his wife's lips. Eric felt like his world was crashing down on him. He had to help.

"We were camping in the forest, and they just came," one of the sons said.

"No, we don't know anything," the father said.

"Well, hell. We need to move quickly if we're going to have any chance of finding her," Chief Hill said.

Eric stepped forward. "I can call Ethan and see if the team is willing to help."

The father looked up at Eric and nodded, gratitude filling his eyes. "Thank you. She means the world to us."

Eric turned to the chief. "Are you okay with me calling Ethan?"

The chief nodded. "Yes, I think that's best. We'll have our guys suit out. They'll be able to move in

41

quickly behind the search team. I'll talk to Ethan and make sure he knows not to approach."

"Sure. I'll be there with them," Eric said, determined to go with the rescue team and look for Claire. Ethan, who the guys called Chaos, had amazing tracking abilities. The rest of the team was good, but Eric valued Chaos's expertise. Claire needed to be found and fast. Who knows what these people had in store for her.

Chief Hill nodded. "Sounds good." He turned back to her father. "We need any information you can give us. Do you have any idea who took her?"

The man was quick to answer. "No, no clue who could have taken her."

For a second, Eric thought he saw something flash across the wife's face, but he didn't have time to question her, and it wasn't his place. He pulled out his phone and dialed his friend, hoping the man was free and there were enough team members in town to go out and look for Claire.

Chief Hill waved to the officer. "Take them to the station and let them talk to one of the detectives. Rice, or maybe Jenkins."

"Yes, sir," the officer said, waving for the family to follow him.

Ethan answered on the second ring, and Eric turned away from them to talk. "Hey, there's a woman who was abducted in the woods. Chief Hill would like the search team to follow and figure out which way they went so the SWAT team can go in and extract her."

Ethan grunted. "I'll find out who can help."

"We'll meet at the station," Eric said.

"Sure."

"We need to move quickly if we're going to find Claire."

Ethan was silent for a moment and then said, "I'll be at the station soon."

Eric thanked him and hung up. He turned to Chief Hill, who was on the phone with one of his guys. After Hill ended his conversation, he hit Eric with a hard stare.

"This is bound to get messy. Are you sure you want in on this?" Hill asked.

Eric gave a sharp nod. "Yes, sir. I need to help look for her."

Chief Hill gave him an odd look before he nodded, then stepped inside to retrieve his car keys. "Let's go," Hill said as he stepped outside.

Eric followed Chief Hill to the station, all the while wondering how scared Claire had to be. From their brief time together, he thought she seemed like a good person. He hoped she was okay. He didn't want their one face-to-face conversation to be their only one.

He gritted his teeth and hoped that they would be able to get her back safely. If these people had done something to her, he wouldn't rest until they paid.

CHAPTER SIX

Eric didn't have to wait long for Ethan to arrive The man was amazing, and though his nickname was Chaos, the man was anything but chaotic. He seemed to exude a sense of competence that put others at ease.

"Hey, man," Chaos lifted his chin as he approached Eric.

"What's up?"

"The woman was taken hostage in the forest by men. I didn't get the exact count."

Chaos glanced around, his lips thinning as he stared into the distance. "I get that she needs to be found, but wouldn't the SWAT team be a better fit?"

Eric's stomach tightened as though he'd been sucker punched. "They—the family—doesn't know where she was taken. Chief Hill wants us to go in and figure out which direction they went."

Chaos nodded. "Makes sense. We will be faster. I'll

go talk to Hill. Zeke, Koop, and Bones are coming with us. Just have them assemble here."

"Sure thing," Eric said.

The rest of the team assembled, and they were ready to head out in about twenty minutes. Chaos was lead, and Eric knew he was lucky to go along with them. These men were the best. He only wished Raid would have been in town so they would have the advantage of having a search dog with them. Then again, they didn't need anyone alerted they were nearby.

Heavy boots crunched on the thick layer of damp leaves and moss beneath them as Chaos led them along the path the family had taken to get to their camping location. This spot was popular for novice campers because the terrain wasn't difficult.

They weren't trying to be quiet right now, but in a few minutes as they approached the campsite, they would make an effort to move quietly. The captors could have taken her far, or they could still be in the area. He hoped they found Claire quickly.

Something skittered off to his left, and he turned, seeing a squirrel jump from one tree to another. He loved living in Fallport, loved how the forest teemed with life. Above, eagles and hawks circled, calling out to their buddies on their hunt. He wished they had a bird's-eye view right now, but a drone wouldn't work well in these woods with all the trees blocking the view of the forest floor. And a drone would alert the captors that someone was on to them.

Chaos paused and turned to face them. "Safety first. We'll determine which way they went and then direct the SWAT team."

"How far do you think they've gone?" Zeke asked.

Chaos shrugged. "No clue. We'll figure it out as we go."

Koop nodded, determination shining in his eyes. "We'll find the trail they took after they grabbed her. The SWAT team is ready to deploy. They'll be behind us soon."

"I hope this works, and we find her. She's too good to be lost to these jerks," Eric said.

"Did you know her?" Chaos asked.

Eric shrugged one shoulder. "I ate breakfast with her at the diner. There were no other seats, and I was more than happy to share my table. She's nice and doesn't deserve this."

"Any clue why they took her?" Koop asked.

"No," Eric said. A weird feeling twisted through him. He had no clue why they would take Claire, but once he found out, he would make sure nothing like this ever happened to her again.

They stepped into the clearing, seeing the tents still up. A few beer cans lay in piles, and the area had a disarray about it. He guessed the place would be considered a crime scene. Maybe Chief Hill would send out someone to collect evidence, or maybe not. They looked around, searching the ground and limbs for any sign of the direction the kidnappers had taken Claire.

"That way?" Zeke asked as he pointed at a path that looked disturbed.

Bones moved in the direction Zeke had indicated and gave a nod. "Lots of footprints. A few broken limbs. This is fresh, too. That storm a few nights ago would have wiped out prints from days ago."

Chaos gave a sharp nod. "Let's go this way and keep looking for signs."

They moved out, going slowly at first. A knot formed in Eric's stomach. If they got this wrong, it could delay Claire's rescue. He wanted her to be safe, but if they went fast and weren't sure this was the path they'd taken her, it would take even longer to find the correct path.

At first, doubt swirled between them, making them all voice their concern. But then they found shoe prints in the dirt and a strip of fabric caught on a limb. After a few minutes, thick underbrush blocked their way. They paused to look deeper, and that's when Eric saw multiple small broken limbs. The people who'd taken Claire had tried to throw anyone following off the trail. But they were smarter than that. They knew to look for even the smallest detail.

As they continued, the trees seemed to close in around them, and Eric had to duck to avoid the low branches that seemed to claw at him. They didn't stumble over a huge root sticking up from the dirt, but there was evidence someone had, possibly Claire.

They kept going, pushing forward in search of Claire, but desperation filled Eric as the day dragged on and the sun started to dip. If they never found her, he knew she would be tortured. They could be torturing her now.

Chaos called a pause after a few hours so they could eat some food and get some water. They had to be on the correct path. He just needed a sign that she was close.

Eric silently cursed the kidnappers as they started back on the path after the break. Anger swirled in his belly. Claire was a good person. Her family had to be filled with fear. The least he and his friends could do was bring their daughter home.

Anger and fear rolled through Eric as they moved lower into a small valley. The trees were tall here, and the underbrush less. Darkness would fall soon, and they would need to take a break and regroup. When Chaos halted them, Eric wanted to keep moving. But as he stilled and the sounds of the forest came into focus, he heard something.

He met Koop's gaze, and they both lifted their eyebrows when the sound of a guy laughing rose nearby. Someone spoke loudly, acting like they didn't care who heard them. Could they possibly think no one had come after Claire? This had to be the men who'd taken Claire.

Chaos made hand motions, indicating they should approach. But they needed to move closer in such a manner the men wouldn't hear them. Eric moved forward until he could see the group. Sure enough, Claire was sitting in front of the fire, her arms bound in her lap. She looked exhausted. His heart went out to her, and he wanted to walk into that camp and take her back. But there was just as good of a chance that he would shoot Claire as there was of saving her. They had to be smart when they went in to save her.

Chaos gave the signal, and they backed up, moving about eight hundred yards away. They could still hear the men, but they couldn't see them. They needed to be quiet, which wouldn't be an issue.

Koop transmitted the coordinates to the SWAT team. The guys on the SWAT team were close to a trailhead not too far away. Koop went back and forth with the SWAT team leader several times, and they decided it would be best to approach at dawn. That meant Eric and the search team would stay out here, watching to make sure the kidnappers stayed in place.

Chaos moved close and talked in low tones so the kidnappers couldn't hear them. "We'll take shifts and keep watch. Koop, you go first. Two hours then wake Zeke. We'll each take two hours while the rest get some shuteye."

"Sounds good," Koop said.

Everyone nodded and moved deeper into the forest, with Koop being the only one staying close. A trickle of relief slithered through Eric, but Claire wasn't in the clear yet. He hated that they had to wait, but it was for Claire's safety. They needed the SWAT team to extract her to keep her from getting injured. He just hoped they could get her out without something bad happening.

CHAPTER SEVEN

The oppressive weight of fear hadn't let up since the men had taken Claire from her tent in the middle of the night. She'd been forced to walk even when exhaustion held her. They'd given her water but not much food. What bugged her the most was that they wouldn't tell her why they'd taken her. She had no doubt her father had done something really wrong, like more than just not paying the guy.

As the sun dipped low, she decided she would have to escape on her own because no one would come looking for her. They'd bound her arms in front of her and forced her to sit in front of the fire. Pain radiated up her legs from her overly sore feet. She wasn't used to walking so far, and moving over the rough terrain had been difficult.

The roots and rocks had tripped her up, and she'd

fallen more than once. She feared what the next day would bring if they forced her to keep going.

The inky black sky above felt lonelier than it had when she'd been with her family. Maybe the intermittent cloud cover that hid the stars or the absolutely crushing fear made the wide-open sky feel threatening instead of comforting.

The men were loud, laughing at crude jokes, leaving her wondering if they would try to take advantage of her. By the time the men wound down, the crickets had stopped chirping, and all the birds had gone silent. All that could be heard was the occasional rustle of the wind and small animals off in the distance moving through the forest.

The hours stretched on endlessly, but she feared sleep. What would these men do to her if she passed out? Already they'd make jokes about having sex with her.

The last of the men settled down on his pack, and Claire watched him, waiting to see if he would sleep. She must have drifted off because the night sky was clear when she woke, and the moon shone above. The moonlight was enough to see that all the men were sleeping.

Though still sore and exhausted, Claire moved to stand. If they woke, she would say she needed to pee, which wasn't a lie. Slowly, she moved away from the fire, praying she could get away from these men.

Something they'd said as they'd joked about having

sex with her stuck in her mind. They expected her father to pay up, and it didn't seem like they were ransoming her. More like her father owed them a huge chunk of money for something they'd done.

Being the person in charge of the books meant she knew about the money, but did she really? Something had felt off since her father handed over the books. It was like some huge chunk of information was just missing. She needed to take a class in bookkeeping and accounting, but right now, that was the last of her worries.

Forcing herself to focus, she glanced around, looking for the best path to take out of the campsite. She moved closer to the edge of the clearing and swore she heard something moving in the forest.

She paused, worried the noise was from a bear or other animal that would hurt her. Tears burned her eyes, but she forced back the tears. Her life was in more danger staying with this group than with a bear.

The forest's darkness wrapped around her as she took one step, then another, leaving the open area and entering one with thick underbrush. Her heart hammered, and blood rushed in her ears, making it difficult to hear.

Excitement began to bubble up as she took more steps, moving farther away from the men who had taken her. She was about ten feet into the trees when something beneath her feet gave way, and the sharp snap echoed through the area.

She gasped, fearing the worst. For a second, maybe two, she had little hope of escape. There was no point in being quiet now, so she took off, moving as quickly as the dark would allow as the men started shouting threats.

"We'll find you, bitch. And when we do, you'll pay."

"I'm going to beat you unless you come back now," one of them called out.

Like that would get her to go back. There wasn't any way she would run back to them. Even the threat of wild animals wasn't enough to make her turn around.

She'd gone about fifteen feet, maybe more, when a hand landed on her arm, yanking her close. She was about to scream when another hand clamped over her mouth. Claire froze as fear twisted tighter. Tears filled her eyes. She didn't want to die.

The hand on her arm went around her waist and pulled her back against a wall of solid muscle. "Claire, stay still," a voice whispered in her ear.

The voice sounded vaguely familiar. It wasn't her dad or brothers. But she knew whoever it was. Or she had heard their voice recently.

"Claire, it's Eric. Don't move. They are coming closer."

Tears stung her eyes as the rush of emotions threatened to overwhelm her.

"Shhh. It'll be okay," he said softly as he held her.

She relaxed against Eric, feeling like maybe she would survive.

A scuffling noise sounded close then the flashlight beam darted over them. Eric pulled her against his body.

"We're fine," he whispered in her ear.

She didn't feel fine, but she trusted Eric. He would keep her safe, or she hoped he would.

Her shoulders relaxed as her captor moved on. A sigh was on her lips when the man turned back and aimed his light their way, shining it on her face. They'd been spotted.

CHAPTER EIGHT

Claire froze as the light stayed on her face. This was it. She couldn't escape. The man with the light lifted his gun and aimed it at them.

Eric stiffened behind her, a groan rising from somewhere inside.

"I've got you now," the man sounded like some lame cartoon villain, but the danger was real.

Panic rose, and she wanted to run, but the gun pointed in her direction held her attention. This man could end their life, and she was helpless.

Eric squeezed her around the waist. "Run to your right."

That was all the warning she got before Eric yanked her to the right, taking off through the low-hanging limbs and scrubby bushes.

The gun exploded behind them, and she let out a yelp. The sound of other men running to the left made them turn more to the right and scramble down the steep embankment.

Claire yelped when her foot hit the water, soaking her all the way through her socks. Each step sent fear stabbing through her. Though the moon was high in the sky, she could only make out the trees and the slope of the land about ten feet in front of her. She needed the sun to see more, but if it was up, then her captors could see them.

"They're over here," someone shouted close by.

Her heart raced with fear. She didn't want to die. They scrambled up the other side of the ravine, running forward to escape the threat.

A cloud blew in, covering the moon. In the darkness, the trees stood like sentries, their branches reaching out to latch onto them, causing them to stumble.

If they couldn't see, then neither could the men searching for them. Eric slowed, and his lips were by her ear. "Quiet."

She nodded, praying they could be quiet enough to escape. Fear had clouded everything, even the words those men had said. They weren't in the clear, but she was thinking now, and she didn't like where her thoughts were going. Her father had owed them money, at least that's what those men had implied. How much money had her dad owed them?

They were going back downhill again, and it sounded like the men were farther away. Then again, they could have just gone quiet but still were following.

A shiver snaked along her spine when Eric put his hand on her shoulder.

"Hold up," Eric whispered.

She paused and wondered what he was doing until he cut the zip strips holding her hands together. She breathed a sigh of relief now that she could move her arms and catch her balance easier.

"Where are we going?" she asked.

"Away from here. We need to get you to safety."

"How did you find me?"

The sound of a branch breaking traveled over the terrain. "Later. We need to keep moving."

He was right. They had to keep moving. The clouds had drifted away, and the moon glistened off the water in a second ravine. This time she tried to miss the deep puddles, but somehow, she ended up soaked to her ankles.

They were moving slowly up the side of a sharp rise. The sounds of people following had lessened. Relief slid through her, but she didn't want to get too comfortable because anything could happen.

When they reached the top of the next rise, she saw that the horizon had turned pink.

"The sun will be up soon," Eric said.

She nodded, hope spreading. "That means we can see better."

"Yes, but it means they can, too. We need a..."

Eric trailed off as his eyes went wide. Claire turned to follow his gaze. Panic set in when she spied the log dropped across a deep expanse. It spanned a gap, and it seemed like there was no way across other than the log. But if they were on the other side, they could escape and be sure no one had followed.

Claire met Eric's gaze, fear causing her heart to race. Her palms grew damp, and sweat trickled down her spine.

"We can do that," Eric said.

She shook her head. There was no way in hell she could walk across that log. "I don't know."

"Let's test it."

They moved toward the log, both of them slowing as they approached. "It looks like it was placed here," Eric said.

Her throat closed as her head began to spin. "I-I don't think this is a good idea."

"It looks secure."

She swallowed over the fear and met his gaze. How was she supposed to know if a log spanning the distance was safe? This was like every nightmare she'd ever had but worse.

Claire inched forward, looking over the edge where the root end of the log sat. It had to be fifty, maybe one hundred feet down. If something happened and she fell, she would be dead.

She backed up, shaking her head. "No. Just no. I can't."

Eric glanced over his shoulder from the direction they'd come. "They are close. We could be dead within the hour if we don't run over this log."

Claire scoffed. "I would never run over that log."

"Okay, walk carefully."

She glanced at the log and then back from where they'd come. They were kind of stuck. They could head down the mountain or circle back around where they'd come, but it would leave them open. If they crossed this log, then somehow pushed it off the cliff from the other side, they could block their path.

She chewed on her fingernail and then remembered she hadn't washed her hands since before being abducted. "I don't know."

"We don't have many options."

Claire blew out a heavy breath. "I'll fall."

"Those men are going to kill us. You can do this, Claire."

Eric held her gaze, his eyes full of trust and encouragement. She didn't know why she believed him, but she did.

He pulled her to him and brushed his lips over hers. When she pulled back, determination flashed across his face. They had few options, and not getting shot was the one she really wanted to go with. But that meant crossing the log over a ravine of certain death.

She hated how her life had almost turned into a cartoon. Nothing about this was normal, yet she was about to walk across a narrow log to the other side of a ravine and hope she didn't fall. If a roadrunner or coyote showed up, she wouldn't be surprised.

"You can do this," Eric said.

She squeezed her hands into fists and gave a sharp nod. This could be the last thing she did.

She felt like throwing up as she inched her way forward, carefully putting one foot in front of the other. The log wasn't as narrow as she'd first thought, but still, there was no room for error.

"You've got this," Eric said.

She didn't feel like she had it. Instead, panic swirled, and deep inside, she knew she was crazy for attempting to cross over this huge gap on a tiny log.

Her stomach dropped when she heard one of her captors yell out. For a moment, she feared he'd seen her, and she had to spread her arms wide to keep her balance as her hips wobbled.

"Go slow. They aren't close. You've got this," Eric said.

Tears burned her eyes, and breathing became difficult. She wanted to cry.

"I don't have it," she said low enough she didn't think he could hear it.

"You do. Keep moving."

She was a little more than halfway across when she heard one of her captors yell out. This time, she knew he had seen her.

"There she is."

Claire squeezed her muscles as panic rose. She had

to make it across. She had about three more feet before she would hit the other side. She didn't want to die.

She had about two feet when the log wobbled. She glanced back and saw Eric on the log, racing closer. He moved at speed, coming toward her faster than she thought possible.

The log began to droop as he moved closer. Their combined weight was too much. Fear had her in its grasp. She couldn't do anything but stare at Eric approaching quickly.

"Move!" Eric yelled at her.

She gulped over her fear and took another shuffling step, then another. The crack of a gun made her scream, and she jumped just as Eric launched himself at the edge of the cliff.

The ground came fast, but it was the hard-packed earth at the top of the cliff, not the trees and whatever lay below at the bottom. They'd survived. But the man shooting at them was trying to change their status as he popped off another shot.

She had done the most terrifying thing she'd ever even contemplated, but it was about to get a whole lot trickier. Dirt puffed up close to her, and she screamed. There was no time to recover. They had to move.

CHAPTER NINE

The sound of gunfire echoed through the woods, and a puff of dirt sprayed on Eric's face. He jerked away, pulling Claire with him. The bastard was shooting at them but not doing a great job.

Panic filled him as his gaze shot to the log they'd just crossed over. His plans of pushing the log off the cliff ledge were the least of his worries now. But if he didn't get rid of the log, the man shooting at them could cross over, and he'd have no trouble tracking them down and killing them. Their options were getting worse instead of better.

"Run," Eric growled as he pulled Claire up and dragged her toward the trees. The man fired again. This time his aim didn't miss.

Pain flashed through Eric, and he stumbled, almost falling to the ground. Claire caught him, pulling him up against her side. Agony exploded through him with each breath. He didn't know if he could keep going.

A desperate yelp escaped his lips as Claire tugged him toward her. He appreciated her attempts to save him from certain death, but the sharp, searing pain ripping through his body was like getting a jolt of electricity. The shock was enough to make his legs nearly useless. Pain twisted through him at an alarming rate, and he didn't think he could make it much farther.

"Come on, Eric. I know you can do this. Keep moving."

He wanted to scream and curse and to tell her to fuck off, but that was the pain talking. She kept them moving past the first tree, then another, and another. He put one foot in front of the other because he had to keep moving. He focused on the earthy scent of dew and rot in the air instead of the coppery blood pouring from his wound.

They'd moved about ten feet, maybe fifteen feet, into the forest when she paused and shoved his back against a tree.

His vision swam as his head pounded. Pain came in waves. His stomach churned, warning him that it might erupt at any second. He had little doubt that if he had eaten anything in the last few hours, it would be on the forest floor.

"I can't—"

Claire grabbed his chin and made him look at her.

Her voice started firm but turned gentle. "I'm going to help you so you can. Listen—"

Right then, before Claire could finish her sentence, a loud, thunderous crack echoed through the forest and was followed by a piercing scream. The crashing didn't stop, and they both flinched. But the tree they were leaning against hadn't moved.

"W-what was that?" Claire's voice shook, and her eyes darted around.

He tried to shake his head, but a sharp pain radiated up his arm to his shoulder. "Fuck, this hurts."

Claire's eyes widened in fear. "I think the tree we just walked over broke."

Her words didn't make sense at first. The fear and adrenaline propping him up had started to fade, and now all he had was pain and dizziness.

"C-can you look and see if he made it over?" he asked with a gasp.

Claire nodded, but he could see the absolute terror in her eyes. Her breathing was heavy and strained. He didn't think she wanted to go look, but they had to know. They were being chased by that jerk, and though the sun was on its way up and would fully rise soon, they were still at a huge disadvantage.

Something sounded behind him, and he jerked with fear. More branches snapped, and it sounded like someone was moving closer. But he had no clue what was coming after them. Before he could move, he had to get this pain under control.

"We need to know," Eric said through the pain and gritted teeth, trying to hold it together.

Claire nodded. "I know. I just, I'm scared."

He reached out with his good arm and squeezed her arm. "I am, too."

"Do you have any first aid supplies in your pack?" Claire bit her lower lip as her gaze shot to the deep gash across his upper arm. He could tell that her face had paled even in the flat early morning light.

"A bit. We need to know if that guy is closing in on us." She nodded and moved, but he reached out, stopping her. "Be careful."

She gave a sharp nod and took off, moving away. Eric sucked in a deep breath, trying to clear his head. Panic rose inside, making it hard to breathe. He would put them in more danger if he couldn't get hold of this pain.

After a few more deep breaths, he forced himself to turn and look at the damage to his arm. Pain flashed hot, making his head swim as he stared at the blood oozing from his arm.

"Shit. Get it together." He pulled at his sleeve, exposing the wound further. He had to draw in more deep breaths to keep himself from collapsing onto the forest floor.

A noise drew him from his inspection, and he saw Claire beside him, her eyes wide and face even paler than before. She shook her head, ramping up the fear shooting through Eric's veins.

"What? Is he close?"

"No. No. He fell. He's trapped halfway down and yelling for help." She paused, worry making her forehead wrinkle. "I feel guilty—like we should help."

"He shot me. He would have killed us both and would do that to us right now if he could. Hell, he came close to killing you. Remember that dirt spraying into your face."

Claire gasped, and he reached out with his good arm, pulling her close. Her shoulders shook as she drew in a ragged breath. A single tear slid down her cheek.

Guilt ate at him. "I'm sorry. I didn't—" He exhaled slowly, the weight of the situation hitting him hard. "Listen, I understand that helping people is in your nature. But honestly, this guy tried to kill you—tried to kill us. He damn near got lucky, and we both could be lying in a pool of blood in the dirt. We have to put distance between us. Once we're rescued, we can tell the police to look for him. But we don't have any equipment to pull the guy out, and who's to say he wouldn't just shoot us if we tried to help him?"

She leaned back, a haunted look filling her eyes. The wind picked up, and her hair blew, framing her face and making her look almost elfin. The urge to protect her almost overwhelmed him.

"No, you're right. He tried to kill us." She moved closer, gingerly examining his wound. "I need to take care of this. What is in your pack?"

He would have to remove the pack, which would hurt like crazy. There was no way he would ever get it back on. "Listen, I think you could move much faster without me. Then you could get help and send them back for me. I—"

"Are you kidding me?" The intensity in her voice sent chills running down his spine. A spark of determination blazed in her eyes, making his insides feel wiggly. She wouldn't leave him behind. He could see it on her face and in her eyes.

He shrugged, sending another wave of pain down his body. "Fine. But I don't know that I can get the pack back on once I take it off."

"I'll carry it." Her voice was firm, but the tenderness caressed his soul. He liked that she wouldn't put up with his bullshit.

"It's heavy. I can't—"

She placed her hand over his mouth, her fingers warm and gentle against his skin. Her strength and determination filled him with hope.

"We'll figure this out together. Don't for a moment think you're getting out of walking back with me. We'll go slow. Those men can't get to us now. They don't know where we went, and their friend fell, so he's of no use to them."

The shouts of the man trapped in the ravine rose, and he saw guilt flash across her face. "There's nothing we can do for him."

Claire nodded. "I get that. I just wish there was something we could do to help."

"We can survive, and maybe he'll live, too. Then when someone who has the proper equipment arrives, they can help him. You and I just need to live long enough to make it back to civilization."

Claire met his gaze and nodded. "I know. I just... I need to patch you up, then we'll figure out how to make it to town. I don't even know which way to go."

Agony lanced through him, and he bit back a sharp cry of pain, trying not to make too much of his injury, but it was taking him down fast. He honestly didn't think the wound was that bad, but the pain was relentless and almost unbearable.

CHAPTER TEN

Claire stared at Eric's arm, trying to school her expression so she didn't give away how bad she thought it looked. It wasn't like she could jump into a car and drive him to the nearest hospital. They were in the middle of nowhere. She didn't even hear any road noise, so there wasn't any hope they could hitchhike to the nearest town.

When her hands had curled around the small first aid kit in Eric's pack, she'd almost groaned. It wouldn't be enough to treat his wound. She would have to make do with the bandages and antibiotic cream available.

Eric flinched as she lightly touched his arm. Afraid that she would only make it worse, she quickly pulled her hands away.

"Sorry," she said, feeling helpless and inadequate. She should have taken a first aid class, but it seemed unnecessary at the time.

"It's okay," he said through gritted teeth. "You need to get it right, or it will worsen."

"I wish I could do more. Your arm should be stitched up, but I don't have any string or anything."

"That's my fault," Eric said with a sigh. "I didn't pack enough supplies."

"Who knew you'd be shot?" Claire asked, trying to put on a brave face. She needed to be stronger and act like she knew what she was doing, so Eric didn't give up.

Eric shrugged and then winced. She hated that he felt bad about anything. He was the one who'd been shot. He shouldn't feel bad about it.

She'd packed enough gauze against the wound to absorb some blood, but they needed to make it back to town. She wasn't sure if an infection would set in or how long it would take before it negatively impacted him.

"You ready to take off?" Eric asked as she finished with the bandage.

"The real question is, are you ready?" Claire asked as concern for him rose. They should stay put, but help might not come if they stayed here. She had lost her phone at some point, and Eric's phone had no service. She'd turned it off to save the battery because if they kept moving, maybe they would find a tower.

Eric glanced around, and so did she. The sun had risen, and though rest might help him, they needed to find help.

"We should move out while the sun is up," Eric said.

Claire nodded. "You're right."

She helped Eric to stand, determined to get them back to Fallport and safety. It didn't really matter to her where they ended up as long as they could find help.

They had walked for about an hour, Eric deciding which way to go. She was glad he could make decisions because she would have walked in circles without him. The dense foliage was hard to get through and slowed them down. Finally, they stumbled upon a thin path. Excitement filled her, and hope blossomed.

"Do you think a town is near?" Claire asked.

Eric shook his head. "No, this path is thin, not two people wide. We may run into someone, but this is one of those paths that extreme hikers take, not people out for a short hike."

"Damn." She glanced around, noticing a drop-off about ten feet away. "What do you think that is?"

Eric stepped over to the edge and glanced around. After a moment, he gasped. Claire moved to look, too.

"What?" she asked.

"I need the binoculars," Eric said.

Claire set down the pack and grabbed the binoculars out of the bag. He held them up with his good hand and shook his head.

"I guess in our path down from the top, we've returned to the area where we crossed over."

"You mean we're walking in circles?" Desperation filled Claire as panic started to set in.

Eric shook his head. "No. We're at a lower elevation, but that's the guy who shot me."

"Can I look?"

Eric hesitated. "He might be dead."

"I need to look." Claire didn't know why she had this intense need to make sure it was the guy, but she had to know.

Eric handed her the binoculars, and she lifted them, seeing the man lying still against the other side of the crevasse. Her lungs froze as she watched him lay there. Guilt snuck in.

"Oh, I feel bad," Claire said, sorrow weighing heavy on her heart.

Eric turned away from the edge and moved back to the path. She followed, hefting the pack to her shoulders. The weight pressed down, making her wish she'd spent more time in the gym lifting weights. No question, this was more weight than she'd ever carried before.

"I should help you with the pack," Eric said, concern lacing his voice.

"No," Claire barked, her voice much harsher than she'd intended. "Sorry. You're injured. I can carry the pack."

"Maybe we could toss some stuff."

"We can decide that later. Besides, some of the heavy stuff is water. I count four more bottles in here."

Eric blew out a breath. "Thank goodness I packed that."

"Yeah, otherwise, we would be totally screwed."

"Come on. Let's move out," Eric said, motioning for her to follow.

They moved lower down the mountain, her hoping they would find civilization soon. She wasn't cut out for this, being lost in the forest. She loved Fallport, but this was a little too much.

The path narrowed and almost disappeared, but they found the trail again after a few minutes of searching. She feared getting them lost even more. She wanted to try the phone again, but the battery was almost dead.

The forest grew dark around them, making it difficult to see. "I didn't think it was so late," Claire said after a moment.

Eric paused and looked up at the sky. "It's not late."

"What do you mean?" Claire asked, confusion filling her. She glanced up, seeing the dark sky.

"Rain," Eric said.

The sky had turned inky black above them. The wind picked up, sending gusts of air through the trees, blowing leaves and pine needles down on them. The scent of rain and electricity filled the air.

Lightning flashed above, and thunder crashed louder than she'd ever heard. Claire jumped and might have screamed.

The wind kicked up in intensity, blowing the tall trees around like they were dancers on a stage. She watched the top of one tree bend and twist in ways she hadn't known trees could.

"Shit, we need shelter!" Claire shouted over the roar of the wind.

Another flash of lightning illuminated the forest and sent thunder rolling, vibrating the ground beneath her feet. The danger was real. They needed to find a place to escape the storm, but where could they go? They were in the middle of a forest, and trees were everywhere.

Despair seeped in, and she felt like maybe their luck had run out. They kept moving along the path, hoping for a miracle.

Suddenly, the path dropped a few feet, sending her crashing to her rear. Pain shot through her body. Then horror filled her as she slid down the slope, crashing into a tree.

CHAPTER ELEVEN

Eric felt like he'd just lost his best friend as he watched Claire disappear down the hill. Panic caught his breath, and he almost stumbled, but he caught himself, sending pain slashing from his arm across his back.

"Claire," Eric called out as he carefully climbed down the steep grade to the trees where she lay still. "Claire, are you okay?"

At first, he didn't hear or see anything, but then he saw her roll just a bit. Her moan made his breath catch. At least she was alive.

"Claire?"

"I'm f-fine. Just a second."

Eric moved to her, wondering if touching her would make it worse. He didn't want to hurt her more, so he kept his hands to himself.

"Can you—" fear seemed to take over. If she

couldn't move, how the hell would they get down this blasted mountain?

"Just give me a moment," Claire said as she moved one arm, then the other, propping them under her body before pushing up.

Eric wanted to reach for her and help, but he needed to make sure she hadn't broken a bone, mainly her back. Heat washed over him, and he nearly passed out.

"Jesus, you scared the crap out of me," he said as Claire shuffled off the pack. She moved one leg so it looked like she was in a lunge and stayed like that for a moment before bracing against the tree and pushing herself up.

"Oh, God. It scared the crap out of me, too."

"Give it a minute and breathe," Eric said.

"The storm."

Eric glanced up, worry filling him. The rain was about to come, and they were already having trouble. The pack was too heavy for Claire and too heavy for him. But they had water and food. They needed to find a clean, dry place to sort through everything in the pack, but he only saw trees and more trees.

Claire straightened and stretched. "Okay, let's move." She bent to grab the pack and moaned.

He reached out and stopped her. "No. I'll carry it."

"But your arm!"

He cupped her cheek. "We work together. That's the only way we're going to get through this. I'll carry the pack for a while, then you can take it. That's how we'll get off this mountain and back to civilization. We're doing it together."

Claire swallowed, and then her lips parted. He wanted to lean in and brush his lips over hers but now wasn't the time. They were both injured, the storm was about to hit, and they needed to find shelter. Later, once they were safe, he could explore his feelings for her.

"Come on, let's go find a city."

Claire nodded though he could see the worry swimming in her eyes. Storms could be destructive, and any rain would make them cold. Hypothermia could set in, making them miserable. They just had to keep pressing forward, and maybe they would stumble upon a town.

They'd walked about fifteen minutes and gone through one spot of rain when the ground flattened out. The trees gave way to a clearing. At first, he thought it was just an empty clearing, but he spied a structure. Claire saw it about the same time as he did.

"Do you think someone lives there?" Claire asked through chattering teeth.

Eric shrugged. The rain hadn't soaked them, but the temperature had dropped enough that the wind had cooled them off. He feared that the only reason he wasn't cold was that an infection had begun to grow and make him hot.

He hoped a jerk didn't live here. The last thing he

wanted was to be shot by some nut who couldn't be bothered to be a decent human.

As they approached the house, he slowed and moved so Claire was behind him.

"Why are you slowing?"

Eric cleared his throat and looked around, trying to judge the area. Lightning flashed, and he glanced up, seeing that the clouds were thicker, darker. They really needed to be inside when the next wave of rain hit.

"I'm going to knock. You stay behind me. I don't want you getting hurt." Claire didn't respond, so he turned to stare at her. Finally, she rolled her eyes.

"Okay. But you were already shot. I don't think you should risk it again."

"I'll be fine. It hardly even hurts now." The lie was hardly convincing, but he couldn't put Claire in more danger. He'd barely had time to process everything that had happened to them, and he was sure Claire hadn't processed half of it. They were in a desperate situation that was scary as hell. Anything could happen.

Eric mounted the steps, noting the rotten wood at the other end of the stairs. Carefully, he made his way up, testing each step before putting all his weight on it. They made it to the door, and he raised his arm when lightning struck so close that he felt the sizzle in his fingertips.

Claire screamed and jumped, knocking him against the door. Pain almost took him down. The door slowly swung open, and he lost his balance. Claire reached out, steadying him.

"Oh crap, I'm sorry," Claire said.

"It's okay. We're inside, and it doesn't look like anyone has been here in a while." He glanced around and spied a lamp. He moved closer and realized it was a battery-operated lamp, not an oil one. He held his breath as he flicked it on. Luck was with them, and light illuminated most of the room.

"That's good," Claire said.

"Sure is." Before removing the pack, he called out. "Hello!" No one answered, but the storm outside picked up, and rain danced on the roof like tap dancers on Broadway.

"I don't think anyone is here," Claire said.

"Let me make sure." He set the pack on the table and sighed in relief. They would have time to go through his supplies and decide what to take and what to leave behind. The cabin gave him hope that a town was close by. Maybe one, possibly two days' walking distance.

He looked around, not finding a telephone or radio. The cabin was sparse and rustic. In the corner sat a cookstove that could be used to heat the room. Luckily the exhaust ran in a pike vented to the outside. He didn't know if it was safe to operate, but he wanted to try.

There were a few pieces of firewood piled against the wall next to the stove. He moved over and was about to pick up a log, but Claire moved in and grabbed the wood first.

"Hey." He narrowed his eyes as he glared at her.

"You need to sit. And I'm not taking no for an answer."

"What about you?" Eric asked.

Claire shrugged. "I'm fine."

He took her by the shoulders and held her at arm's length. "We need to work together. We can't do this if we lone wolf this. You and I are a team."

Claire's gaze didn't waver as she stared up at him. He could almost see his words working through her mind. He wanted to pull her close and kiss her but resisted the urge.

"Listen, we're both injured."

She bit her lower lip then her face relaxed. "Then let's talk through what we're doing."

He nodded. "Okay. That sounds good."

"I'm not used to people working with me."

Her words made him pause. "What do you mean?"

"Well, like I said, I work for my family, but it's more like my dad just tells me what to do, and I do it. I don't work with them on anything. I'm stuck in a back office and don't talk to anyone throughout the day. Actually, I don't really know what he does. I mean, I know what the business sells, but I don't know what he does on a daily basis. I don't know what any of them do. It's weird."

"What's weird?" Eric asked.

"I get the feeling that they don't want me there. Like, they'll stop talking if I come out of my office."

Eric kept quiet, not sure he liked what Claire had said about her family. He knew she loved them, but from everything he'd seen, he thought they were taking advantage of her. Maybe later, after they escaped this hell, he would talk with her about her family. She was such a nice person, and he wanted her to have a good life.

His gaze strayed over her as they worked together to start the fire in the stove. He was attracted to her, but thinking they could have something would be presumptuous. Maybe they would just be friends. If he could help her have a good life, he would be satisfied. Who was he kidding? He wanted her in his bed, but it was too soon to think like that.

At least the smoke seemed to be venting properly and not filling the cabin. After the fire was going and warmth started to expand from the stove, he moved to the pack and pulled out a bottle of water and a protein bar.

Claire moved close and took one of each, her lips quirking up into a smirk. "Let's sit and eat."

"Sure. The couch?" He eyed the couch, wondering what surprises awaited them from the thing.

Claire shrugged. "It doesn't look too bad."

"It's old, but you're right. This place doesn't have too many surprises." Eric moved to the couch and kicked it. Nothing ran out from underneath the couch frame or cushions.

Claire's lips quirked up. "You ready to sit, or do you want to kick it again?"

Eric rolled his eyes. "Sit. I think it's okay."

They settled on the couch and opened their protein bars. He needed help and didn't balk when Claire reached over and opened the wrapper for him.

"Thank you."

"You're welcome."

They ate in silence, the rain pounding on the roof above. He was thankful they'd escaped the worst of it. He wasn't sure how they would have dealt with being out in the rain.

"This is good," Claire said.

"Yeah. It's not the worst place I've been holed up in while on a mission."

Claire nodded. "You know," her voice was barely above a whisper, "those men who kidnapped me mentioned something about my father."

He waited for her to say more. After a long moment, she still hadn't said anything. "What did they say about him?"

She shook her head. "I don't know. Maybe I'm blowing it out of proportion."

"If you feel like something is off, talking about it won't hurt. It may actually make it better." Maybe he shouldn't be pushing her to talk. They were still in a desperate situation, and this might upset her more.

He wouldn't push again. If she wanted to talk, she would.

After Claire finished her bar and took a sip of water, her eyes narrowed like she was thinking hard. "I love my parents and my brothers. They are my family, but some things have made me think."

"Like what?" He pressed his lips closed as worry wound through him. She needed to reveal this in her own time. The last thing he wanted was to force her to talk about something she wasn't ready to reveal.

She blew out a breath, and her eyebrows pinched together. He didn't want to push her away, so he wouldn't ask again. But he had a bad feeling about her parents. Even with the pain rolling through him, he sensed her parents weren't on her side.

"So I do the books, and it feels like maybe there's something I'm missing."

A warning went off in his head. He said nothing, fearing she was involved in some weird illegal activity.

"Maybe I should have told my dad no when he demanded I do the books. I don't know enough about accounting or bookkeeping. I just do what he tells me to do and try to make it work." She shook her head and then rolled her eyes. "I'm probably making too much of this, but something seems off."

His stomach tightened. He didn't know Claire well enough to know if she could trust her senses, but he trusted his, and something was very wrong. "So what did the guy who took you captive say?"

Claire stood and moved to the stove, adding a small piece of wood to the fire. She spun and met his gaze before looking up at the ceiling. The rain had slowed, but it still pounded against the roof.

"The guy said something that almost sounded like he had been working with them. My dad, I mean. Like he knew trouble was coming and didn't do anything to protect us." Claire's frown deepened, and then she threw her hands up. "I sound ridiculous. Like, do you even think that's possible?"

He shrugged, trying not to respond too harshly. He wanted to yell and scream, telling her that her father was probably laundering money or running some kind of scheme. Blowing up at her wouldn't help them in this situation.

Claire was in a tough spot, and if she didn't know what was going on with her father and his business, she could actually be in legal trouble. Somehow, he needed to convince her to stay with him instead of going home. She could end up in real trouble if she left with her parents.

CHAPTER TWELVE

Claire blinked open her eyes and found that her head rested on Eric's shoulder. His soft snores puffed against her cheek. Happiness, excitement, and maybe a little lust twisted through her.

She needed to pee, so he had to move. She flexed, tightening her muscles, which was a mistake. Pain slithered down her body, and she grunted. Yesterday's tumble was coming back to remind her that she wasn't a superhero who could recover fast.

Pleasure that they'd fallen asleep together filled her. She hadn't slept with many men. Actually, she'd only spent one night in another guy's bed, and that had been a friend. Their friendship turned awkward after that.

Carefully, Claire moved away from Eric, not wanting to wake him. She studied the bandage on his arm, thinking it might have stopped bleeding. At least there wasn't blood dripping from the bandage.

She took a slow step and lifted her arms over her head, trying not to gasp as pain hit her again. When the pain cleared, she glanced back to the couch and saw Eric open his eyes. A jolt of energy shot through her as their gazes connected.

"Morning," he mumbled. Did he regret sleeping with her—not that they'd actually slept together in a coupley way, but they'd just been asleep in the same place at the same time.

"Morning," she said, feeling a bit of awkwardness filter through.

He yawned, stretching his one arm up as he lifted his legs, rolling his ankles. He glanced around as he sat forward, groaning as he moved. "What time is it?"

"No idea," she replied.

He groaned, making her think he really was in pain. "We should probably get moving."

Claire nodded, wishing they were in a relationship because this man made her feel things. She wanted the open conversation they could have if they were together. Right now, there was so much she wanted to say, but she feared his reaction.

She turned from him as heat traveled up her neck to her face. If she said anything more, she would end up embarrassing herself. This man wasn't here to date her. He'd only been tossed into this situation because someone her father knew had abducted her.

The windows were covered with a film of pollen

and dirt, so she couldn't see outside, but some light filtered in, indicating the sun was inching up, eating away at the darkness. They needed to get moving, and hopefully, they would make it back to civilization. Storms popped up all the time, and they had no cell service, so they didn't know what today would bring them.

Eric came out of the bathroom, his skin looking a little pale. They really needed to get to a doctor. They had no antibiotics, and he had to be hurting. She'd found some over-the-counter pain pills in his kit, but that would barely be enough to take the edge off.

"We should eat before we head out," Eric said.

She nodded, trying to act cool and calm and not like she'd just spent the night snuggled up next to a gorgeous man who had saved her from certain death. "We should. I wish we knew where we were."

Eric pulled out a bottle of water from his bag and handed it to her. She took it gratefully, drinking deeply. When she set the bottle on the table, she noticed he still watched her. His gaze jerked away, and he busied himself with something in his pack.

Heat filled her again. Why had he been staring? She probably looked frightful. She lifted a hand and touched her hair, trying to smooth it.

"So what do we have for breakfast?" she asked, aiming to keep her tone light but thinking she failed miserably since her voice sounded breathy instead of calm. She was a mess. This man wasn't into her. He was just here to rescue her and take her back to civilization. If she didn't keep reminding herself of that, she would make a fool of herself.

His lips quirked up on one side. "More protein bars."

"Oh yum." She chuckled and reached for one of the bars. "Seriously, though, I'm glad you have these. Otherwise, we'd starve."

He nodded as he tried to open the tight foil package around the bar. She took his bar, careful to not brush her hand against his, and opened it for him.

"How do you feel?" she asked as worry spun through her. She hoped he was strong enough to walk today. There was no way she would abandon him, but she would be little help if he passed out. He didn't seem too bad off, but she knew how untreated infections could take a person down.

Eric shrugged and then winced. She felt for him. He had to be hurting something terrible. Her pain was mostly manageable. Her muscles were sore, and her back ached, but that could have been from sleeping on the couch. The fall yesterday had hurt, and the couch hadn't helped, but sleeping on the ground would have been worse.

She took a bite of the protein bar, keeping her worries to herself. The bars weren't great, but it was better than going hungry. She and her family weren't prepared to be lost in the wilderness. Then again, she hadn't expected someone to attack them. That still bugged her. Why had those men showed up and attacked her family and then taken her hostage? What was her father into?

They finished their bottle of water, and she used the restroom again. At least the place had a well and some sort of septic tank, so they weren't using an outhouse. At least, she hoped the waste was dumped into a septic tank.

Eric had taken a few things out of his pack, leaving them three bottles of water, two bars each, some of the first aid kit, and extra jackets. Everything else would be left behind. He wasn't leaving much behind, but the pack was a few pounds lighter.

"I can carry it for a while," Claire said.

Eric shook his head. "I'll go first, then we'll see."

"I'm okay. I wasn't shot. If you pass out, we're done for."

Eric blew out a ragged breath and shook his head. "I'm fine for now. I've taken a few pills, and we'll switch in a bit. But you're in pain, too."

She nodded, trying to find the words to make him see that she could carry it. "I am in pain. But it's not that bad. And I really need you to stay upright all day. If you drop, there's no way I can find a town or other people to help. You're the only reason I haven't walked around in circles all day."

His lips thinned, and she could see the moment he realized she wouldn't back down. "Fine. I'll let you carry the bag first, but we're switching every hour. And if you seem to be having issues, we'll switch before."

She nodded, hoping they found some help before too long. "At least we've finished off some of the water. I know we need to be careful and conserve it, but I'm glad that weight is gone."

"Yeah, that's good," Eric said as he opened the door to the cabin, and they stepped out.

The sun was up and peeking from behind the trees, splashing long shadows across the meadow. She sighed and took in the beauty.

"Why the deep sigh?" Eric asked.

"I love this place. The trees, the raw beauty. I mean, heck, the sunrise is gorgeous, and it's probably just a typical sunrise, nothing special to most people in this area. But to me, it's amazing. I don't want my memories of this landscape to be so negative."

"You know, you can love an area and hate what happened there at the same time."

She shrugged, "I know. I just... I don't want to be bitter. I'm processing things. Like my dad. Why did those men attack us?"

Eric didn't say anything for a long moment. After a while, she glanced over, and it looked like he was deep in thought.

"What are you thinking?" Claire asked.

He met her gaze and shook his head. "I don't know

what is happening with your father. I'm sure you'll figure it out once you reconnect with them."

His words didn't make the worry go away. She had a sinking feeling that her father had done something wrong.

They'd changed the pack three times already, and it was Eric's time to take it when she turned to stretch and look at the path they'd come from. That's when she noticed that the sky behind them wasn't blue.

"Shit, that looks bad."

Eric turned, his lips thinning as his nostrils flared. "We need to pick up the pace."

She met his gaze and shook her head. "You're already going as fast as you can."

"I'm fine."

She rolled her eyes. "No, you're not. Just admit you're having a tough time."

His eyes narrowed. "You don't let people get away with BS, do you?"

She scoffed. "If that were true, I wouldn't be here."

"What do you mean?" Eric asked as he hefted the pack, trying to hide the pain that was obvious to her.

"I think my dad was doing something illegal, and I don't know enough about bookkeeping to have caught it. I should have stayed at school and kept studying or gotten a job somewhere else. I think I'm to blame for some of this."

Eric reached out and grabbed onto her shoulder,

squeezing. "You are not to blame for other people's actions. If your father did something, that's on him."

"But what if I did something illegal?" Real fear threatened. She didn't want to go to jail for something she'd done. She should have said no when her father demanded she quit the university and come home.

"Like what?" Eric asked.

"I don't know, but..." She trailed off, not wanting to voice the fears because it would make it real.

Eric didn't push for more, and she appreciated that about him. After another thirty minutes, the wind picked up. Now, the air seemed thick with the promise of rain. She thought too much about her father and what he could have done. It had to have been a mistake. Her father was a good man. She remembered something he said about storms, about how storms served as a reminder of the fragility of life and how it was important to be prepared. Guilt assailed her. She'd been so quick to doubt him, to think he was up to something illegal.

"What is it?" Eric asked as they came to a split in the path. They both stopped and looked around.

Claire shook her head. "Nothing."

"It's not nothing," he said. "Come on, tell me."

She sighed, looking up at him. "I've been too hard on my dad. I feel guilty for thinking he's doing something illegal."

Eric nodded. "I think you need to look into it once you get home."

"Do you think I'm making stuff up?"

Eric's lips thinned. "I don't know. I wish I had the answers for you. Now, there's this split. Which way should we go?"

Her eyes grew wide as shock twisted through her. "No idea. I've never been here."

"Neither have I, and I admit I'm tired, and that storm worries me."

She glanced back and noticed how much closer the storm was. Concern filled her. This time there wasn't a cabin for them to hide in. They would be exposed to the elements, and they seemed to be no closer to civilization. Eric's face had gotten paler, and he was walking slower. They needed help.

"I don't like this," Claire said.

But before Eric could respond, she heard a noise up ahead. Claire's heart stuttered as two figures emerged from the trees. They were dressed in dark clothing and had a wild, menacing look.

Claire felt a wave of fear wash over her. She reached out and put her hand on Eric's arm.

"Who are they?" she whispered.

"I don't know," Eric said, his voice low and hushed.

The men stopped and stared at them. Were these men who had taken her hostage, or were they people out for a hike? Her fear increased as one of the men adjusted the shotgun at his side. She wanted to run, but where could they go? They were lost, a storm was approaching, and now they were facing two men with guns.

Thunder rolled in the distance, reminding her they were caught between a rock and a hard place. The rain was just a passing storm, but she couldn't help feeling that it symbolized the chaos in her life.

CHAPTER THIRTEEN

"Follow us," one of the guys called out.

Eric didn't know if they should follow or not. They didn't know these two men, and they had guns. So much could go wrong.

Another round of thunder rolled over the mountain, and Claire jumped beside him. They didn't need to be out in the storm. So much could happen. They'd almost been struck by lightning yesterday, but following these men could lead to harm.

"Hurry up. That storm is coming fast." The man waved them to follow.

Fear churned in his belly. He didn't want to make the wrong decision, but they had little choice. He wasn't feeling good. Claire had guessed, but she didn't know how bad he felt. He was dragging and schlepping the pack was getting to him.

"Should we follow?" Claire asked.

Lightning flashed close by, and thunder cracked so hard they both jumped. He didn't think they could not follow.

Eric nodded and held out his hand. "Let's go."

They stayed about ten feet behind the men. He didn't want to get too close out of fear. Maybe he was too suspicious, but he didn't trust these guys. The pain might have made him more paranoid, but why were two men out here in this weather?

It didn't take long for the rain to start. And it wasn't a gentle rain. This was a full-on body-soaking downpour. His clothes were soaked in a matter of minutes.

Lightning lit up the sky, and thunder crashed, but the men didn't seem to care; they kept walking. Despite his fear and doubt, Eric knew they had no choice but to trust and follow these strangers.

About twenty minutes later, Eric spied a house through the trees. It wasn't the cabin they'd stayed in the night before. This house had a wrap-around porch and was two stories tall. Civilization had to be close.

Eric only hesitated for a moment before moving up the steps to the porch. The men removed their jackets and boots, and Eric and Claire followed their lead. He worried that maybe he should keep his boots close, but they were caked in mud, and he didn't want to track the dirt into the house.

Eric could tell the men were older than he was, but not too old. Though the men had shotguns, they weren't threatening them.

The taller of the men seemed to sigh as the rain let up. "Have you been out in the storms for long? Looks like you don't have a tent."

Eric shook his head. "We don't. I'm with the local search and rescue group. We went out to rescue Claire." He paused and pointed at Claire, who swallowed hard as the men narrowed their eyes at her. "Things didn't go as planned."

"Are you bleeding?" the shorter guy asked.

"He was shot," Claire said.

"What?" Alarm filled the taller guy's face.

Eric nodded. "We just need to get back to town. Is there one close?"

"A few hours' drive, normally. A tree fell in yesterday's storm, and we can't get through."

"I'm surprised you were out in the weather," Claire said.

"Are you injured, miss?" the tall one asked.

"I'm okay. I'm worried about Eric."

The tall one nodded. "I'm Merit, and this is Bruce."

"Nice to meet you." Claire held out her hand for them to shake but winced when she fully extended her arm.

Merit's lips thinned. "Let's see what we can do." Merit opened the front door, and a wave of calm hit Eric. Neither of these men threatened them. It seemed like they were good people.

He stepped into the house and glanced around. The house wasn't packed with furniture, though it looked nice and homey. Two recliners were set up for watching TV. There was a small dining room table, four chairs, and a hutch full of multiple China patterns.

Bruce nodded at the hutch. "Merit's mother insisted we take the China since we're the only one in his family in a stable relationship."

"Ah," Eric said as even more peace came over him. Looking more closely, he spied multiple photos of Merit and Bruce at parades or just out on the town.

"Nice place," Claire said.

"Thanks," Bruce said. "We like living out here. I'm a doctor but retired."

Claire's eyebrows shot up. "But you're young."

Merit chuckled. "He says he's retired but spends about six months out of the year treating people in low-income areas. He's only retired from his private practice, not from doctoring people."

"Over the wire, I heard there was a fight in the woods. I guess that was you two?"

Eric nodded. "Yeah."

"Do you know if those other men were caught?"

Merit shrugged. "I don't know the details."

Bruce shot them a smile. "Let me get a look at your arm."

"Sure," Eric said.

Merit waved for her to follow. "Let me show you to the bathroom. We have some sweatpants and other clothes you can wear while we wash yours."

"Thank you," Claire said.

"I'll take a look at you after I finish with Eric," Bruce said.

Eric felt a wave of relief wash over him. He had been worried about his injury but hadn't wanted to say anything to Claire. Now they were both safe. Or he felt safe.

"Thank you for taking care of this—of us," Eric said.

Bruce nodded and motioned for Eric to follow him. They made their way down the hallway, past a library, something that looked like an office, and a laundry room that looked space-age compared to his washing machine. They entered a room that looked like an old-timey doctor's office.

"This sure is one interesting setup," Eric said.

Bruce chuckled. "Merit thought it was funny. But now, he's thankful we have it. A few of the long-time residents show up here from time to time. One of the local women had her baby here last month. She couldn't make it to town and needed medical help."

"Wow, that's amazing."

Bruce had Eric remove his shirt. "Can I just strip out of my jeans, too?" Eric asked.

"Sure. We have some sweats you can pull on while we wash and dry these. Even if we call for help, no one will make it out here for at least a day with the storms coming in."

"Is it bad?" Eric asked.

"Sure is. It should rain all day and into the night. I'm glad we found you."

"Yeah, me, too," Eric said.

After removing his jeans, he took the pair of sweats Bruce offered and pulled them on before sitting on the exam table.

"I need to sterilize the area. It will probably be easier if you lie back."

Eric shrugged. "Sure."

Bruce helped him lie down and then examined the area. After a moment, he met Eric's gaze. "Are you allergic to any medicine or latex or anything?"

"No, sir. I'm not."

Bruce nodded and then moved to a locked cabinet. He grabbed supplies and placed them on a metal table. Before moving closer, he washed his hands and dried them with a clean cloth.

"I'm going to give you a shot for pain and an antibiotic. Are you taking any medications?"

Eric shook his head. "No, no medication. I had two Tylenol tablets a few hours ago."

Bruce nodded. "We should be okay then. After the pain shot sets in, I'm going to really go in and clean the wound, and then I'll stitch you up. It's going to hurt."

Eric nodded and blew out a breath. "I'm good."

"Awesome. I want to clean out as much dirt as possible in this situation. Then once you get back to town, you should see a doctor."

He nodded and watched as the doctor gave him the first shot, then the second.

"Okay, let that set for about ten minutes so your arm goes numb."

"Thank you," Eric said. Bruce left the room, and Eric shut his eyes and rested. Maybe he fell asleep, or Bruce was quiet, but suddenly the man was back beside him, preparing to clean the wound.

It took Bruce about ten minutes to finish cleaning the wound and start stitching it up. Claire came in, followed by Merit.

Merit nodded at Eric's arm and the handiwork Bruce had done. "Looks like you're almost done stitching him up."

Bruce nodded. "Almost. A few more stitches, and I'll be finished."

"I'll call the police and tell them we found you."

Eric felt relief that Merit was going to call the police. At first, he hadn't trusted these men, but now he knew they were good. They'd lucked out. He wasn't sure how much longer he could have kept going. Worry for Claire filled him, but for now, they were safe.

"Thank you," Claire said.

Merit's lips tipped up in a smile. "Sure. We love helping people."

"Okay," Bruce sat back and stared at his handiwork. "I'm happy with the results. And now we can get you up and grab some food."

"Food sounds good," Claire said.

Merit stepped into the room and held out his phone to Claire. "The police wanted to speak to you."

Claire's eyes widened, and her hand shook as she held it out for the phone. "Sure."

Worry twisted through Eric. He hoped her family was still safe. With the questions Claire had, if her parents had been attacked, it would only open more questions.

CHAPTER FOURTEEN

After eating their fill of chicken, potatoes, and vegetables, Claire yawned and stretched. She wished she was at home. If she was, she would curl up on her couch and fall asleep to reruns of one of her favorite shows.

The police just wanted to make sure she was okay. She told them about the man who'd fallen in the ravine and about where they were. She was happy to learn the search and rescue team had found the guy and pulled him out. The search team had to break during the storms but planned to go back out to look for them. They were glad she and Eric were safe. Hearing that everyone in her family was okay had brought relief. Now she just had to figure out if she should stay working for her dad or if this was a sign.

It felt good being in this house with these two men. She was safe, and they weren't out in the rain The shower had been amazing, making her feel refreshed. But the refreshed feeling was gone, and exhaustion was creeping in.

"I think you two should turn in for the night," Bruce said.

Eric sighed. "I'm exhausted."

"Let me help you clean up." Claire moved to stand, but Merit put his hand on her shoulder.

"No way. Go upstairs and get some sleep. You've had a long day."

Guilt filled her, but he was right. She was exhausted. They were running on fumes and had been for a while. If they didn't rest, their bodies couldn't heal. She was happy to head to bed.

Eric stood and moved to step away from the table, but something happened, and he reached out and grasped onto the chair.

"Are you okay?" Claire asked as worry filled her.

He waved her off. "Yeah, just a little tired."

"Let me help you upstairs," Merit said.

Eric shook his head. "You've both done so much. I can manage."

"No way," Bruce said. "We're helping you up."

Eric shrugged and gave in to their help. Eric shuffled up the stairs, his arms draped over Bruce and Merit's shoulders for support. Claire followed closely, anxious as she watched Eric slowly move up each step.

The aroma of the food they'd cooked mixed with the

antiseptic smell from the doctor's office and cleaning fluids downstairs, but up here, the medical scents were gone, and something more floral filled the air.

Eric groaned when they finally made it up to the second floor. She glanced around, taking in the paintings hanging on the ecru walls.

Worry for Eric grew as she took in his pasty complexion. The man was strong, but being shot and not having the wound treated for more than a day had drained his strength.

Bruce opened the door to the bedroom and led Eric in. Claire noticed the gray upholstered chair in the corner, the antique wood dresser, and the four-poster double bed.

She drew in a slow breath, wondering where she would sleep. Did they have another room? She thought she should be in the same room as Eric to check on him, but she wasn't sure they should sleep in the same bed.

"Here you go. If either of you needs anything, we'll be downstairs. The bathroom is through here." Bruce pointed to a closed door.

Should she ask where she was going to sleep? No, she could sleep in here. It would be fine. Eric was a good guy. She could tell he was by everything he'd done for her so far.

Merit stepped over to the door and then pointed at the bed. "I hope sleeping together won't be a problem.

We didn't focus on making guest rooms out here. This is the only other bedroom other than ours."

Claire shook her head. "That's no problem. Thank you. This is great."

She wasn't sure how Eric felt about them sleeping together, but she felt an odd mix of excitement and fear. She trusted Eric but also knew her heart was already drawn to this man and actually sleeping in a bed with him would mean something.

Bruce and Merit left the room, shutting the door behind them. Her stomach tightened, and her head spun. She was making too much out of their sleeping arrangements.

"I can sleep on the floor," Eric said.

She shook her head. "No way. We're both adults, and we can do this. Let's get ready for bed."

Eric's gaze sizzled over her skin before he glanced away. She breathed out a sigh of relief. They barely knew each other, but her feelings had grown since meeting him in the diner. That felt like a lifetime ago. Maybe they wouldn't develop a relationship, but she couldn't deny her attraction to this man.

Claire pulled the comforter over her, grateful for its warmth. It had been a long day, and she was exhausted, but she couldn't sleep—not with Eric lying so close to her.

The room was dark, but enough light spilled in through the lace curtains that she could make out Eric's profile. She watched his chest rise and fall in rhythm with his breathing, thankful he was still alive and safe. The gunshot wound had brought them together, but she'd grown to care for him more than she'd ever expected in such a short time.

Her heart ached at the thought of what would happen after this ordeal. She hated that their relationship was based on danger and chaos. What if it ended badly?

Tears stung her eyes, but she blinked them back, refusing to cry. She'd insisted that he brush his teeth first, and he'd fallen asleep before she finished in the bathroom. She was glad he was sleeping. Her heart ached for the pain he was going through. He'd only been trying to help her and gotten shot for the effort.

There had to be more going on with her father though she didn't know what it could be. She would need to figure everything out once she returned home.

She closed her eyes, letting the stress of the last few days ease away. Right before she drifted off, a loud noise made her jump. Eric reached for her, his hand landing on hers.

"Just thunder. Go back to sleep," he mumbled.

She'd assumed he'd been passed out, but maybe he was just as much a light sleeper as she was. It didn't take long for her to drift off, and when she woke in the morning, the sun shone through the lace, illuminating the room with the soft morning glow.

She stretched, and the door to the bathroom

opened. Eric stepped out and met her gaze. A smile flashed across his lips.

"It's all yours."

She groaned and sat up. "You look better."

"I feel better. I think the infection is almost gone. My head doesn't ache, that's for sure. I'll be downstairs. The guys left our clothes on the chair, so you can get dressed."

"Wow, I didn't even hear them come in."

"Right? I slept right through it. I do remember you jumping after the thunder."

She nodded, a little embarrassed that he'd been awake for that. She shuffled into the bathroom and almost gasped at how awful she looked. Her hair stuck out from her head and looked incredibly knotted. She needed to shower and spend some time on her hair.

She glanced into the shower and found conditioner as well as a good shampoo. At least she could fix herself before they left.

Her body still ached, but the pain was much less. Clean and dressed, she headed downstairs and ran into Merit.

"You look much more rested today."

"Thank you. I feel better."

"Good. We have breakfast almost ready."

"Thank you so much. I can smell the coffee, and it smells delicious." Though she loved being out in nature, she really appreciated the comforts of a house. Maybe living in this area would be too much for her, but then again, she wouldn't be abducted and taken hostage every day.

The dark, rich coffee tasted like heaven, and she felt much better after eating. Just as she took her last bite of bacon, the sound of tires on gravel filtered in through the open window.

"Must be the police," Bruce said.

Relief filled her. She'd liked spending alone time with Eric but was ready to return to civilization.

"I should use the bathroom," Claire said as she stood. When she caught her reflection in the mirror, she breathed out a huge sigh and shook her head. Whatever had caused those men to abduct her couldn't really be her father's fault. She knew her father was a kind and honest man. At least, she thought he was. There had to be some mix-up. This couldn't be her father's fault.

After she finished in the bathroom, she opened the door and bumped into Eric. He reached out to steady her and then pulled her close, hugging her with his good arm.

"I'm glad we're being rescued, but I did enjoy spending time with you."

Shock pulsed through her. Eric lowered his head and brushed his lips over hers. She opened for him, reveling in the feel of his tongue sliding against hers and the way he held her close so their bodies melded together.

The loud knock at the front door pulled them apart.

He held her gaze and then nodded before stepping into the bathroom. What did that nod mean?

She didn't have time to think about it. The police were here to rescue them, and they needed to return to Fallport.

The drive back to the city was made mostly in silence. She didn't know what to say, and it had turned awkward with the police in the car with them. Fear that her father was doing something illegal twisted through her. She hated this feeling. It was like she was about to get caught doing something wrong, though she had no idea what it could be.

Claire hated that she kept ping-ponging back and forth between thinking her father was totally innocent to thinking he'd done something wrong. She wanted facts because her feelings were strongly in the innocent category as far as her family was concerned.

Before going to the station, the detective dropped Eric at the emergency room, telling him to get better. She had no time to say goodbye or ask questions about when she would see him again. Dissatisfaction filled her as they drove away.

When they approached the police station, Claire wondered if she should ask for a lawyer. Not that she'd done something wrong, but the fear twisting in her guts wasn't because of the men who had attacked, but what truth she would find once she talked to her dad.

Claire's mother ran out of the station and grabbed her in a tight embrace. The crushing hug felt good. It had been ages since her mom had hugged her so tightly.

The scent of her mother's perfume wafted around them, and she sighed. This was where she was supposed to be.

Her mother pushed her to arm's length, tears glinting in her eyes. "I can't believe you're okay. I was so afraid."

"I know." Her mother pulled her close again. The overwhelming warmth of her mother's embrace left her on an emotional edge.

Thoughts of Eric filled her mind, and discomfort at being with her parents wafted in. She wasn't the same woman who had walked out of Fallport into the forest a few days ago. Too much had happened, and too many questions needed to be asked.

Now wasn't the time. Once she got home and had some alone time with her father, she wouldn't hold back. She needed to know if her suspicions had any basis in fact.

As her mother led her to the van they'd rented, she glanced back, wondering if she would ever see Eric again. She hoped she would, but she had to focus on what was ahead of her.

CHAPTER FIFTEEN

.

The plane touched down in Baltimore as the sun gave a
final fiery red-orange blaze as it sank below the horizon. So much had happened since the day they left
town, and she'd experienced so many emotions, too.
Excitement, happiness, wonder, then fear, worry,
doubt, and now the gnawing dread that had settled in
her stomach. She didn't want to think too long about
the tangled mess of financial data she would have to
tackle once she returned to work.

They escaped the airport only to be dumped into a
snarl of traffic. She felt a little lost and overwhelmed,
unsure if she was ready for what lay ahead. She just
wanted to be home and in her own bed—scratch that.
She wanted to take a long shower—no, bath—and then
snuggle under the blankets and forget the last week.
Not all of it. She wanted to remember Eric. But would
he ever want to see her again?

She hadn't really said goodbye. She'd thought she would have had time to have one last goodbye, maybe see if he wanted her to come back down in a few months. But her parents had taken over, and she'd been whisked away. She hadn't even had to sit for questions from the police. That had been very strange. She'd asked about it, but her dad had brushed it off, saying not to bring it up.

The oddest thing was her parents pretended like everything was normal. Once they'd loaded onto the plane, they'd all acted like nothing nefarious had happened in the woods. Her body was still aching from being abducted, then chased, and almost killed, but her parents didn't want to hear anything else about her ordeal.

They wanted to act like their family hadn't been targeted, but beneath this façade was a truth they knew but no one spoke of. She had to find out what was going on.

Once home, she took a bath, then crawled into bed and snuggled under her covers, but still, her mind couldn't push away the worry. She had to know. Before anyone else in her family was awake, she dressed, grabbed a muffin from the freezer, and headed to work. Every noise made her jump, and she almost lost it when a garbage truck drove past, but she was able to keep it together and work more instead of abandoning her desk and hiding until someone else showed up in the office.

She dug through file after file, looking for information, when she stumbled upon a hidden file she didn't think she was supposed to see.

When she clicked, a password box popped up. That would have been the end of her digging before being taken hostage, but she'd almost lost her life, and she had to know.

Claire crept over to the door of her father's office, looking around like she thought someone might see her. The building was empty, and they didn't have cameras anywhere on the property. No one would know she'd entered her father's office.

She held her breath as she pushed open the door, worried that her father would suddenly appear or maybe an alarm would go off. Nothing happened.

Her breath caught, and her stomach twisted, but she forged ahead and entered his office. She clicked on a light and jumped even though she was the one who had turned it on. A tight chuckle bubbled up, but it had nothing to do with her finding something funny. Instead, it was everything to do with worry and fear.

Her stomach tightened, and she bit her lower lip, struggling to come to terms with the way she was violating her father's privacy and the need to figure out if he had roped her into doing something illegal.

She didn't want to go too deep into bashing herself for following her father's instructions, but she should have known.

Tears burned the back of her eyes, but she pushed

them away. She didn't know for sure that they were doing anything wrong. This could all be some sort of misunderstanding.

Claire didn't know where to look for the passwords, but she suspected it wouldn't take her long to find what she needed. She was right. In less than ten minutes, she had all the passwords she needed for her father's accounts and documents.

She'd always believed honesty and following the rules was the best policy, but she had to figure this out. If she didn't, they could all be in serious danger. Before leaving her father's office, she made sure everything looked the way it had when she entered.

Armed with photos of the page of passwords and accounts, Claire returned to her computer. It was still before four in the morning, so she would have hours to look through the material and figure out what was going on.

Once she had the financial documents open, she noticed something strange. The numbers were too calculated, too meticulous, and didn't match the numbers in the other file. A knot formed in her stomach as she realized her father was hiding something.

Claire stared at the phone on the desk and thought about calling Eric, but it was only six thirty. He might still be asleep, and she didn't want to bug him. She spent the next hour going over everything she'd learned, figuring out just how bad what they'd done was.

By the time she heard the door open, someone had stepped in. She knew she was in deep trouble. The money numbers she had for her father's business weren't real numbers. Instead, her father had used her to manufacture a set of books that didn't show everything. She'd been duped into creating legitimacy for his company though their business was anything but legitimate.

CHAPTER SIXTEEN

Claire sat across from her father, trying to remain calm. She'd given him time to settle before she'd come in here but had no doubt this wouldn't go well.

"So what is this about, Claire Bear?"

When she was five, she'd liked the nickname, but after realizing her father hiring her to do the books had been a cover, one that made her guilty, it pissed her off. If the police, FBI, or whoever investigated white-collar crimes came in and looked at the books, Claire would be the guilty party. Or that's what they'd initially think. It would take a long time to get everything sorted out correctly.

"We need to talk," Claire said.

Her father narrowed his eyes and glanced away before looking at her again. Did he look guilty? She wasn't sure.

"This sounds serious," he said.

"It is serious." Fear whipped through her. What if she was wrong? She'd reviewed the files, looked at all the numbers, and found evidence of her father forging her signature, making it look like she'd been the one to fix the books. She hated this, hated that she had to say anything.

"Listen, I'm sorry you were caught up in that misunderstanding. I swear—"

"Hold up," Claire cut him off. Her heart sank as she stared at her father, wondering how he thought her almost being killed was a misunderstanding.

"I said I was sorry," he repeated, his voice heavy with emotion. "I know you're angry, and I don't blame you. But it's really not that bad."

Claire's throat tightened. She had a feeling he wasn't going to accept responsibility. "I know about the money laundering," her voice was barely above a whisper.

Stunned that she'd led with that, Claire cleared her throat and adjusted in her seat. She hadn't meant to spill the beans so quickly. Her father opened his mouth and then closed it. His cheeks turned red then he shook his head.

"No. I don't know where you're getting that data, but I'm not."

"I saw the files. You're—"

Her father jumped up and pounded on the desk. "Shut up. You snooped. I should—"

Her dad didn't finish the sentence as Blaine opened

the door.

Claire turned to the door and then back to her father. He threw his hands up in the air and raced out. Silence sat heavy, and she stood slowly.

Blaine moved to block her exit. "You don't know what you're talking about."

She narrowed her gaze and stared at him for a long moment. "You knew?"

Blaine shrugged, and her heart felt like it crashed to the floor. She couldn't believe what she had just heard.

"Does Mike know?"

Blaine rolled his eyes. "What do you think?"

She felt like her heart had been ripped into pieces at the betrayal. Her family knew she had been implicated in the company's documents for being corrupt with their money. The way the files read, she'd devised a scheme to launder and embezzle money. Her family had betrayed her, and she had no choice but to believe it. She could see it in her brother's eyes.

Claire pushed past Blaine and headed to her desk. She had to fix this but didn't know how. The documents her father had forged were hers to copy now, so she copied them onto a flash drive, wondering if she should do more. She didn't want to turn her family in to the police, but what options did she have?

The men who had taken her hostage had done so because they knew her father had been stealing from them. At least, that's what she'd assumed based on the papers she'd read and the emails she'd found. Her life was still in danger, and she didn't know if she could ever fix this.

After she'd copied most of the files, she saw her father headed her way. She didn't have everything, but it would be enough to clear her name.

Before her father was close enough to see what she was doing, she disconnected the thumb drive and unplugged it, slipping it into her pocket before he got to her.

"Listen, that didn't go the way I wanted it to. I didn't want you to find out this way," he said. "I was hoping to tell you after I'd made things right. I'm so sorry, Claire Bear. I'm close to getting everything under control."

Claire stared disbelievingly, her mind racing and her heart heavy. Anger surged through her veins—at her father, the situation, and herself. She'd trusted her father, relied upon him, changed her life, and returned to the family business instead of pursuing her passion in school.

Betrayal, confusion, and guilt all rose to the surface, clouding her thoughts. Her father had made her look like the guilty one, but why? She shook her head, not knowing what to do.

"How long have you been doing this?" she asked.

Her father shrugged. "Does it matter?"

"Yes, it matters to me." Tears stung her eyes. Had he been doing this, using her, for years? "How long have you used my name to hide what you were doing?"

"It wasn't my idea," her father's words were a knife to her heart.

"So you've been taking money from innocent people and using me as a scapegoat since the beginning?"

Again with a shrug. "I was desperate and needed the money to keep our family afloat. You wanted to eat, right?"

"Yeah, but I don't want to go to prison because you decided to do all your illegal activity under my name."

"I can't go to prison. It would be easier on you," her father said.

Shock pulsed through her. "You're fine with sending me to prison."

Her father shrugged. Claire was taken aback by her father's nonchalant response and stared at him in disbelief. She expected a debate or an argument. His shrug seemed like an insult.

"And what about the money?" she asked. "Where has it all gone?"

"We have accounts overseas."

Claire felt a surge of both rage and confusion. She had thought her father's intentions were pure, and to find out that he had been manipulating her for years was overwhelming. She was furious, yet at the same time, part of her wanted to believe he had acted in her best interest. Her stomach churned as she tried to make sense of the situation.

"Why did you use me?" she asked, her voice trembling.

"You're a girl. If we were caught, your sentence would be less. You'd probably get off with a slap on the wrist."

Claire felt sick to her stomach. Her father's words echoed in her head. "You would have let me go to prison just to protect yourself?"

She felt the warmth of anger mixing with confusion and disbelief. She could barely process what she had heard. His betrayal felt like a physical punch to her gut. How could he do this to her?

Her mind raced as she tried to come to terms with the reality of the situation. Now she wanted to throw up. Her father was fine with sending her to prison so he could escape responsibility.

"Come on, it wouldn't have come to that. No one knows what we're doing." Her father's assurances felt hollow.

"The men who abducted me knew."

"Yeah, but they are doing illegal shit, too. They won't talk to the cops."

"But if they found out, I'd look guilty. I'd be the one going to prison instead of you."

Her father looked taken aback like she'd said something crazy. "Well, I can't go to prison. I can't risk it."

She felt like she was in a nightmare. "What are you going to do now?"

Her father sighed and looked away. "I don't know,"

he picked a piece of lint from his pants and then glanced up, meeting her gaze. "I suppose I'll have to find a way to make things right."

"When you say you want to make things right, do you mean to make sure I'm not implicated if the cops show up?"

He shrugged again, making her feel like she would never escape what he'd laid on her. If anyone ever investigated this company, she would go to prison. There was no way she would ever look innocent.

"Look, I'm sorry you feel like you were wronged, but family is important. You do things for your family. That's how it is," he said.

Claire's stomach tightened. Everything she'd thought she knew was wrong. She'd trusted her parents to love her, but this wasn't love. She'd never given her permission to be used like this. She had no say in her name being used to do illegal activity. Even if the cops figured out she'd been thirteen when some of the paperwork had been signed, they would still toss her in jail. She felt like she was in a daze, not quite sure what to do.

"I need to think," Claire said as she stood. She almost reached for her pocket to make sure the thumb drive with the evidence was still tucked inside, but she fisted her hands, praying her father didn't ask her to empty her pockets.

"Okay, Claire bear, but know we only wanted what was best for the family. Family is everything, and sometimes we have to do things to help out, things we don't want to do.

With a curt nod, she scrambled to pull her jacket on. Her hands shook with anger and worry and a huge dose of betrayal. She probably didn't need the jacket now that the sun was up, but she wanted the security it offered.

Before leaving, she met her father's gaze. She wanted to speak, to find some common ground with him, but the bitter taste of betrayal made her words hang in her throat. Emotion for the man she once loved flooded her, but she couldn't trust this man.

She wouldn't be safe at home or anywhere in the city. An image of Eric flashed in her mind. Maybe it was ridiculous to head back to Fallport, but she felt like it was the only place she would be safe.

CHAPTER SEVENTEEN

Eric stepped out into the evening air, the hazy glow of the setting sun casting an orange hue over the world. He stopped by a pillar and leaned against it, staring up at the sky. So much had happened in the last few days. He closed his eyes, trying to find solace in the silence. Eric's heart felt heavy as he thought of Claire. Why hadn't she come to say goodbye?

It didn't matter. He straightened and pulled out his phone, arranging for a ride-share to pick him up. He tried to focus on the positive. He was alive. His arm would heal. The bone hadn't been hit, and he could return to work sooner rather than later. Bruce had done a great job cleaning and stitching the wound, and the doctors here thought he looked good. There was no reason to open him up again.

Before the car arrived, his thoughts drifted to Claire. She'd changed something inside of him. He should text her and find out if she was okay, but she'd lost her phone, and he didn't know if she'd gotten another one.

The car arrived, and he got in, making small talk with the driver. At home, he settled in for the night but still felt unsettled. Worry for Claire grew. He wondered if she was at home. Did she feel safe? What if those guys went after her again?

Her suspicions of her father made him worry. Had her father engaged in illegal activities?

Eric was pretty much a straight shooter. He might have nicked a candy bar when he was a kid, maybe taken gum from his friends without asking, but he'd grown up and learned it was wrong to take what didn't belong to him. He learned to respect other people and their property.

In the Marines, he'd met all types of people and learned that the honest men and women went further. The ones who fucked around found out that stealing another person's equipment got noticed. He saw what real punishment was.

If her father actually had done something wrong, he hoped Claire didn't have to pay the price for his stupidity. She'd already spent too much as it was.

The next morning he got up, ready to head to work. He wasn't sure how much he could do, but he wanted to try.

The house he'd been working on was closer to being finished, but there was still work to be done. Five trucks were parked near the front of the house, and he spied two guys he knew heading inside.

The project's foreman, Desmond, waved him over as he stepped from his truck. "Hey, if it isn't the man. I heard you were shot. How are you feeling?"

Eric shrugged. "Sore, but I'm okay."

"Let's start you off small."

"I can handle—"

"Hey, you don't know what you can do. We'll start you on something easy. Just go with it. I can't have you getting hurt on my job."

Eric nodded, knowing Desmond was right. If he got hurt, he would screw this up for Desmond.

The first task he was assigned was helping Vince measure and cut the chair rail in the dining room. It amazed him that they were this far along. The last time he'd been out here, there hadn't been any sheetrock on the walls, and now it was all up. Then again, the sheetrock guys worked like crazy.

"Good to see you," Vince said as Eric stepped into the hall where he'd set up his tools.

"It's good to be up and moving around."

"This job shouldn't take too long. Though, they do have the wood on the walls in multiple rooms. I like doing the dining room first."

"I'm good with whatever we do."

"Sure, sure."

Vince started measuring on one side of the room, and Eric started on the other. Everything was going fine until he reached out to grab a pencil he'd dropped. Pain shot up his arm to his neck, almost making him drop to his knees.

"You okay?" Vince asked.

"Yeah, yeah. I'm good." But he wasn't. The pain still pulsed through him and wasn't going away.

Eric worked for another thirty minutes until the pain was too distracting, and he couldn't get the measurements right. He'd almost cut wrong, and he hated wasting materials.

He leaned against the wall catching his breath. Maybe he should head home and get some rest.

"Hey, Eric, you should go," Desmond said as he stepped into the house. "You look pale, and we can't have you dropping out here."

He lifted his hand to acknowledge the boss.

"Sorry. I thought I would be able to keep working."

"Hey, you were shot. None of these guys have ever been shot before. Go get some rest and come back in a week. I know you're a great carpenter. Take some time and get some rest."

Eric nodded. He wished he could stay because he liked working, but Desmond was right. If he got injured or injured someone else, he wouldn't ever get hired again. He wasn't desperate for money, so taking off didn't hurt that bad. He just wished he could stay and work.

He was driving through the middle of town when he saw Brock's truck at On The Rocks. He didn't need to drink, but it would be nice to talk to the guys. He'd texted them but hadn't seen any of them since he'd made it home.

He parked and pulled out his phone, wondering if Claire had picked up a new phone. She hadn't texted or called, so he doubted she had a way to contact him.

He got out of his truck and stretched before heading into the bar. A few of the regulars were already there, nursing beers and sharing stories. Eric glanced around and spied Brock and Drew sitting at a table close to the bar. Zeke was behind the bar, along with Hank.

"Hey, Eric, how are you feeling?" Zeke called out when he saw him.

He waved as he headed to the table with Drew and Brock. "I'm good. A bit sore. Too sore to work."

"Aw man, that sucks."

"Hey, Eric," Drew said as he approached.

"You having a beer?" Hank asked.

He shook his head. "No, I'll stick to tea so I can take a pain pill later if I need to."

"Sure. I'll have it right out."

"How is your arm?" Drew asked.

He rolled his shoulder and winced. "I'm still hurting."

Drew's smile faded. "I hope you get better soon."

Zeke came out from behind the bar with his tea. "Here you go. So how is Claire?"

"Thank you. I have no idea how Claire is. She left without saying goodbye."

Drew leaned in and lowered his voice. "I heard the cops wanted to question her, but her parents took off with her, not allowing the cops to talk to her at all."

Eric's stomach dropped at that news. "That's odd. I was wondering what happened."

Drew's brows furrowed. "It is weird that they left without letting the cops talk to her."

Eric nodded. A chill ran down his spine. Claire's doubts about her father circled his thoughts. Maybe he should say anything.

"Do you know something?" Drew asked.

Leave it to Drew, the ex-cop, to pick up on his worries. He shrugged and sipped his tea as he tried to figure out the words he wanted to say.

"I don't know if I should say anything."

"None of us are currently in law enforcement, but we could have ties that can help her."

Eric nodded. He met Drew's gaze and then glanced around, making sure no one was paying them any attention. "While we were out there, she began questioning if her father was doing something illegal. It took her time to go from trusting him explicitly to questioning everything."

"What do you think, based on what you saw?" Drew asked.

"I don't know. I don't trust her father. But I have

nothing to go on other than the worry I saw from Claire."

Drew's lips thinned, and he gave a sharp nod. "I'll look into it and see what I can find out."

Eric nodded. "Thank you. That would make me feel better. I don't know what to think, but I hate the idea of Claire being in danger."

Eric finished his tea and decided to leave since he was feeling tired. Every medical professional had told him he needed to take it easy, but he'd tried to work and do everything he normally did. He had to take time to heal.

Once home, he pulled out his phone and stared at Claire's contact information. A sense of dread settled in his chest. He needed to figure out the best way to contact Claire. He feared what would happen to her if she didn't have someone looking out for her.

CHAPTER EIGHTEEN

Claire rushed out of the office, anger swirling in her belly. What would her father do? She had the evidence that she'd been betrayed in her pocket, but would that be enough?

She didn't want to go to the cops, but what if her father turned her in, or worse, what if something happened and the FBI just showed up? Were they already watching her father and his company?

A sense of dread filled her as she approached the house she'd lived in for the last few years with her family. They'd shared meals, laughed, argued, and loved on each other in this house. But all the love, the caring had been a front. Her father had betrayed her, and that cut like a knife.

As she walked through the door, taking in the entryway and the dining room, a wave of sadness hit her. Her heart sank as she started packing her few items she didn't want to leave behind. Luckily, her parents had shown her how to stash money, and she had an excellent hiding spot where five thousand dollars sat under the floorboards. She would have enough money for a while so she could decide what to do.

She reached for the thumb drive, making sure she still had it. The drive was safely tucked in at the bottom of her pocket.

She closed her eyes as doubt swamped her. What if she was wrong? What if her father was right, and even if someone investigated, she wouldn't go to jail? She was young, and her father wasn't. He would die in prison, but she would get out in a few years and be able to make a life…as a felon.

She didn't want to be a felon and have to put up with restrictions for life just because her father had used her name in his illegal activities. She didn't think she should pay for what he'd done. But family was first. She'd heard that for years.

Torn between wanting to stay and help her family and running so she didn't end up in prison for her father's illegal activity, she had to make a choice. But the options available to her sucked. Once she left, abandoning her family, she wouldn't be allowed back in the fold.

She zipped up her bag, looking around at what was left of her old life. She had to walk away and not look back. The love she had for her family chiseled at her heart, but the betrayal she felt shielded her from the worst of the pain of leaving.

Fear twisted through her as she raced out the front door and down the steps. When she saw the street was clear and her father and brothers weren't waiting for her, she breathed a sigh of relief.

She didn't have her phone with her since it had been lost in the woods. No one could track her that way. It was crazy that she had to run from her family, but she needed time to make decisions.

She spied a store across the street as she approached the bus stop. She headed over, knowing she needed some way of contacting Eric. A cheap burner cellphone would work.

She didn't have his number, but someone in Fallport had to know him. Once she arrived in the quaint town, she would set about searching for him.

After purchasing the phone, she stepped out of the store, smiling to herself. The happiness faded as she realized she needed to figure out how to get to Fallport. She could rent a car, but that would leave a trace, same with purchasing a plane ticket. Maybe she could take the train.

She'd bought a phone with data so she searched for train schedules and found a train leaving in about two hours that she could take to Virginia. Then it was only a short bus ride from Lynchburg to Fallport. She could be in Fallport by morning.

Excitement buzzed through her. She had a plan to

leave, but as she waited for the bus to the train station, doubts crept in. What if Eric didn't want her in Fallport? They were acquaintances, not friends. He may not accept her being with him. What if he decided he didn't want anything to do with her?

So many questions and fears swirled through her mind. She was abandoning her family for a stranger. No, that's not why she was leaving. She'd walked away from her father because he'd betrayed her. She couldn't trust him. If the FBI had shown up before her abduction, she would have ended up in prison. At least now, she was armed with the knowledge that she'd been framed.

Filled with anxiety and uncertainty, she bought her ticket to Lynchburg and waited for the train to be called. Her stomach tensed, and she realized she hadn't eaten anything when she got a little dizzy. She'd been so upset about her father and how he'd blamed her for his illegal activity she'd forgotten to grab food.

When the announcement went up over the speaker that it was time for her to board, she made her way to the track and waited patiently.

She had bought a regular ticket, not first class or business, so she was seated at the back of the train. She didn't mind, though, since the car was mostly empty.

It didn't take long for the train to start going. Fear hummed in the back of her mind, making her wonder if her father would show up and force her to go home. But she'd escaped Baltimore.

The view out the window wasn't great. The area around the tracks was some of the worst in Baltimore. She wondered what living in a place like this would be like. Her family had money, but that money came from her father stealing it and doing illegal stuff. She didn't hate her life, but if her father had given her a choice, would she have picked poverty and living somewhere like here and not one of the nice neighborhoods.

She didn't know. She'd never been given the option. Instead, her father forced her into the situation they were currently in.

She drew in a deep breath, trying to stay calm as the train chugged south. Once the meal car was open, she quickly grabbed something to eat and returned to her seat. This was the first time she'd ever traveled any distance by train. She felt weird, like she didn't belong, but she knew she didn't belong with them because of how her family had used her.

Maybe this was always supposed to happen. Leaving her family behind was hard, but she had no other good options. She just hoped Eric would help her, and she would finally feel like she had a place to be herself.

CHAPTER NINETEEN

The bus's brakes squeaked as they came to a stop. Claire sat up, wiping the sleep from her eyes. She'd been traveling all night, and what little sleep she'd gotten hadn't cleared her exhaustion.

She glanced around, a smile playing on her lips as she realized she was in Fallport. No one had shown up to stop her. She was really free.

As she exited the bus and grabbed her bag, tightness settled in her chest. The town was small, nestled deep in the Appalachian Mountains, where everything seemed to operate a little slower but seemed so much richer.

Everything seemed much more peaceful here than it was in Baltimore. Maybe it was just the lack of people, or possibly it was more.

The air was cleaner out here, the sky bluer. The

trees stretched tall into the sky, and the ground felt more stable. There were no fast-moving trains or subways, and fewer cars and people. Fallport called to her soul, making her feel things she didn't know she could ever feel.

After she left the bus depot, Claire glanced around, trying to get her bearings. They hadn't spent much time here in town, but the place seemed familiar.

She thought the diner was to her left and took off that way. She had gone a few blocks when she paused and glanced around.

"Are you lost?" A woman pushing a baby stroller paused to talk to her.

"Oh, I—" Claire paused and glanced around. "I guess I am. I'm looking for the diner—Sunny Side Up."

"Oh, gosh, I love that place. I gained so much weight eating their pancakes when I was pregnant with her. You're going the wrong way, though."

"Thank you so much. If you hadn't stopped, I don't know that I ever would have found it."

"I'm Sophia, and this is Daphne."

"It's nice to meet you. I'm Claire."

"I can't help but notice your bag. Are you visiting?"

Awkwardness swirled. Claire didn't know how to talk about what had happened. Tears sprang to her eyes, and she swiped them away fast, worried this woman would think she was a total mess.

Sophia's eyes went wide. "Sorry, I didn't mean to

dig. You don't have to tell me anything. I didn't mean to pry. When I came here, I would have freaked out if someone had asked me questions. I left a bad relationship and found a great community here. I'm just saying that if you ever want to talk, you know you have someone here who will listen."

Claire's eyes burned. She had to look away so she didn't burst into tears. How had this woman known something bad had happened in her life?

"I didn't mean to make you cry," Sophia said.

Claire shook her head as she choked out a bark of laughter. "No, don't apologize. Seriously, you are spot on. I can't talk about it now, but I'll keep you in mind."

"Let me give you my number."

Claire stopped walking and shook her head. Sophia stopped, and a worried look crossed her face.

"I'm pushing you again. I'm sorry."

Claire held up her hand. "No, you're not. I'm just shocked that you're being so nice. Not you specifically, but that anyone is this nice. It's so different."

Sophia reached out and squeezed her hand. "This place is different."

They exchanged numbers when they were across the street from the diner. Claire couldn't believe she'd run into someone who was so nice. She hadn't expected to meet anyone, let alone someone so kind.

Claire crossed the street, excitement filling her at the thought of seeing Eric. The likelihood of him being in the diner was low, but she didn't let that spoil her enthusiasm.

After freshening up, she sat at a table near the bathrooms where she could see almost all the room. Eric wasn't here, and most of the breakfast crowd had cleared out.

"Hey, I remember you," Lisa said as she approached.

Claire smiled. "Hello. Your name is Lisa, right?"

"Yes."

"I'm Claire."

Lisa flashed a smile before she narrowed her eyes. "How about pancakes today?"

Claire gasped. "How did you know I wanted pancakes?"

"I saw you talking to Sophia. That woman ate so many pancakes and said they were like a religious experience. I thought she might have told you to get some."

Laughter bubbled up. "She might have."

"Pancakes, and how about a scrambled egg and bacon so you have some meat to balance the sweet out?"

"That sounds great."

Lisa grabbed a mug for her and poured coffee before heading to the kitchen to put in her order. More customers had left, and now only two more tables had people sitting at them.

Worry slid in, making Claire wonder if she'd made a huge mistake. She had the money for a hotel and should probably make a reservation. It was silly for her to think she could have stayed with Eric, even if that's exactly what she'd wanted to do.

The door opened, and she jumped. A young couple came in, and disappointment wove through her. She needed to get a better grasp on reality. Finding Eric wouldn't be this easy, and even if she found him, that wouldn't mean they would have any type of relationship. He may have saved her, but that's as far as their relationship had gone.

She needed to have better expectations. When she finally ran into him, she needed to have a better plan than some crazy woman hunting him down.

Lisa brought over her food, and she thanked the woman profusely and dug in. The first bite of pancakes was nearly magical. She agreed with Sophia that these pancakes were amazing.

After a few bites, she realized the food she'd consumed on the train hadn't been enough. She ate like she was starving and hadn't eaten in months.

She finished the eggs, bacon, and a healthy portion of the pancakes.

"Well, you were hungry," Lisa said as she came by to clean up the table. Her eyes narrowed. "Do you need more? Maybe a slice of pie."

Claire shook her head. "No, I couldn't. I'm stuffed. I was hungry. I...I didn't have a good day yesterday and didn't eat much."

Lisa nodded, then grabbed the carafe of coffee and

poured another cup for her. "You sit here as long as you need. The lunch rush doesn't start for another few hours. If you want, I can watch your bag while you freshen up in the bathroom."

"Thank you. I might take you up on the offer."

Lisa moved to another table and took care of the customers. Claire sipped her coffee, her thoughts going from what she'd learned about her father and the company. She couldn't believe her father had forged her name on documents, so it looked like she was guilty of embezzlement and money laundering.

After she finished her coffee, Claire asked Lisa to watch her bag for a moment. She needed to make some decisions. Her money wouldn't last long, especially if she lived in a hotel.

After she left the restroom, she checked the diner, seeing that all the customers had left. It was just her, Lisa, and the cook in the back.

"Hey, sweetie, did you need anything else?" Lisa asked.

Claire blew out a breath and decided it was time to ask some questions. "I need a job, a place to live, and I need to find Eric."

Lisa's eyes went wide and lit up. "I can't help with the first two, but I know how to find Eric."

Claire felt a surge of excitement. "Oh, that's great."

"I'm off in an hour and can walk you over to his friends. They will be able to get you in contact with him."

"That would be great." Her stomach tightened, and her palms grew damp. Worry pushed in, making her think he wouldn't want to see her. Maybe he wouldn't, but she couldn't pull back now. She was here and might as well tell him she had arrived in Fallport. If he didn't want to see her, she would find out later.

Lisa came to her table when she clocked out, her smile wide. "Are you ready?"

"Yes. Thank you for being so kind."

"Sure. Kindness is the best policy."

Lisa's words were shocking, though they shouldn't be. Kindness should be how everyone operated. She followed Lisa out the door and down the street, walking on the wide sidewalk. The town seemed just as magical as it had when she'd first arrived with her parents.

"Oh, we're here," Lisa said as they stopped in front of a bar.

"This place?" Claire asked. Was Eric a heavy drinker?

"They aren't open yet, but one of his buddies owns On The Rocks. His name is Zeke. Let's see if he's in there. If he is, Zeke should be able to tell you how to contact Eric."

"Oh."

Lisa laughed. "You were worried, weren't you?"

She shrugged. "Maybe."

"Well, Eric seems to be one of the good ones. I don't

know him really well, but from what I've seen, he's a nice guy."

Claire nodded, trying to control the excitement buzzing through her. Lisa opened the bar's door and called out.

"Hey, Zeke, you in here?"

A gruff voice confirmed he was inside. "What do you need?"

"A friend of Eric's is looking for him."

Lisa stepped in, and Claire followed, worry filling her. She feared that Zeke wouldn't tell her how to contact Eric, or maybe Eric would tell Zeke to make her go away. All sorts of problems sprang to mind.

Before she could chicken out, Zeke stood before them, wiping his hands on a towel.

"Eh, you must be Claire."

Shock coursed through her. "You know my name?"

"Yeah. The guys have been talking. Glad you got free from that jerk holding you. The cops still want to talk to you."

Fear slid down her spine, and the urge to run almost overwhelmed her.

"Oh."

"About the kidnappers. They just need information," Zeke said.

Claire nodded, wondering how talking to the cops would go. She knew her father had broken the law and was a criminal. But if she turned him in, she would have to face possible charges, though she hadn't done anything wrong.

Maybe coming here had been a huge mistake. She might just end up in more trouble here than she would have at home.

CHAPTER TWENTY

Eric awoke with a start, his body tense and ready for action. Then, he remembered—he was on hold for at least a week due to an injury sustained while protecting Claire. Despite his body's protests, he would do it all again in a heartbeat. He wanted to know if she was safe, and the only way to find out was to call.

Claire hadn't reached out to him yet, but Eric had to trust that she could take care of herself. Reaching for his phone, he composed a message, carefully choosing his words before pressing send. He had to know if she was okay, but he also respected her independence.

Now that his phone was tucked safely away in his pocket, Eric was determined not to obsess over her response. He busied himself by tidying the house and making breakfast before settling in at the computer. After answering emails, he pulled up a browser window and started to type in Claire's family name.

Before he hit enter, he wondered if he should be doing this search anonymously instead of in a regular browser. He didn't want to believe that her father could be involved in something dangerous, but he had to play it safe.

He switched to a more anonymous method of searching and typed in her father's name and the city they lived in, desperate to find answers. He combed through the results, trying to find anything that could help him locate and protect Claire. At first, he found nothing, but he changed a few search parameters and found enough to make him afraid for Claire.

He grabbed his phone, disappointed she hadn't texted him back. Maybe she hadn't bought a replacement phone. Then his thoughts went dark. Or what if she was in danger? He needed to find her and figure out if he could help. What was the best way to contact Claire?

His stomach tightened. What if she didn't want his help?

He could drive to Baltimore, and then what? He had the address to her father's company. But it could be dangerous. He'd been shot, too, recently and wasn't moving fast enough to be useful in a crisis. If he was at one hundred percent, he wouldn't hesitate. Heck, he'd been sent home from work because he couldn't do his job. He needed to find someone to help him.

He was about to call one of the guys when his phone rang. He saw it was Zeke and paused. Had the man read his mind? No, there was no way Zeke was calling to say he would go to Baltimore to rescue Claire.

Eric answered, tamping down the urge to blurt out his request to be accompanied to Baltimore for a rescue mission.

"Hey, what's up?" Eric asked, trying to sound cool and calm as possible.

"Eric, that woman you rescued from the forest."

Panic filled Eric. Was something wrong? "Yeah?" His throat closed with fear and dread.

"She's here in my bar."

A wave of relief washed over Eric as the panic ebbed away. He could get to Claire safely. "What? She's there?"

"Yeah." The phone line crackled like Zeke had tried to cover his mouth. "Want me to send her away?" The question was muted, and Eric knew Zeke hadn't wanted Claire to hear that question.

"Not at all. I need to see her. I'll be there in a few." Eric's lips spread into a wide grin as he ended the call. Excitement pumped through him at the prospect of seeing Claire.

He jumped up but had to reach out and grab the table to steady himself. He guessed his injury was still affecting him. He breathed deeply, pushing back the pain and dizziness, and searched for strength and control.

He wanted nothing more than to leap into his car

and race to Claire's side, but he knew he needed to take a moment to refuel. Snatching up a protein bar and a glass of water, he gulped them down. The energy boost settled through him, clearing his head so he could focus. What was she doing in Fallport? Would she stay or leave as quickly as before?

CHAPTER TWENTY-ONE

Eric pulled up in front of Zeke's place and jumped out of his car, his heart pounding in anticipation. Had she really returned? He needed to calm down. He didn't know why she was there. Since leaving the hospital, he'd wanted to hear from her. She'd gone through so much, and now she was back here.

What else had she endured to make it back to Fallport? He wasn't deluded enough to think she'd come back for him. They hardly knew each other though he felt like he knew her better than anyone else.

He paused before stepping into On The Rocks. The lights were on, erasing the shadows that made the atmosphere of this place. His gaze swung from the left over the center of the bar to the right, but he didn't see Claire. Had this been some sort of setup?

"Hey, how are you feeling?" Zeke asked as he came out of the back room.

"Honestly, a little lost," Eric said.

Zeke's lips tilted up, and he shook his head. "She's in the bathroom. She'll be out in a few. Looks like she's had a rough few days."

Eric didn't want to ask what Zeke had meant. What did a rough few days look like? If she was physically okay, he'd take that as a win.

Thoughts of him forcing her to run over that log filled his mind. That log had fallen soon after they'd both gotten across. It had been dangerous, maybe even reckless, but their options had been few.

That man would have killed them both if they hadn't escaped him. Heck, being shot wasn't some fun party. At least it had been on his left side, not his dominant one. At least he'd eventually be able to work. His overhead lifting ability would be worse, but he hadn't died, and he would be able to get back to work in a few weeks.

The squeak of the bathroom door filled the place. At night with the music going, he never heard that, but that sound shot through him, making his throat squeeze. Claire was heading his way at this very moment.

What could he say? He didn't want to play this off as nothing. She had come back to Fallport. There had to be something about it. Maybe it was just the area, the land, and the beauty that had made her return, but he thought there might be more. Maybe she wanted to see him.

If she wanted him—no, he wouldn't allow himself to get worked up. She wasn't here for him. She'd come back because she loved the area.

She was looking down at her hands when she stepped out from the hall leading to the restrooms. At that moment, Eric knew he wanted to do everything possible to make her his, but he had no right to force it. His feelings had developed in the few days they'd been together. It had been a fantasy or some weird syndrome from being trapped in a desperate situation with her. He wanted to spend time with Claire, wanted to see her smile, hear her laugh, do hard things with her and enjoy life. He had it bad.

Claire glanced up and froze, her eyes going wide. He was thankful the bar was empty except for Zeke. He hadn't known what he expected, but Claire rushing to him and flinging herself into his arms hadn't been it.

"I don't want to hurt you."

He shook his head. "You couldn't hurt me."

Her left eyebrow cocked up, and that one move made his balls tighten. Already he was half hard, but he'd been fighting the attraction.

She rolled her eyes and then moved to his left side, gently touching his forearm. "Does it hurt much?"

Her hand on his skin burned, but not because of the pain in his arm. He shook his head and then turned. His good hand rose to her face, and she glanced up, surprise flaring. He froze, worried she didn't want anything from him other than friendship.

They were standing there, him almost touching her, her chewing her lip like she was nervous.

"Are you okay?" he whispered.

Tears filled her eyes, and he couldn't keep his hands off her. Instead of cupping her face, he pulled her close, wishing they knew each other better. He wanted to know everything. Why had she returned, and how long was she planning on staying?

The front door of the place opened, and laughter spilled in, followed by too much talking. Eric grabbed her hand and led her back to Zeke's office.

"Hey, are you…" Zeke trailed off.

"Someone decided you all are open." Zeke rolled his eyes. "Shit, I guess we're starting early."

"We're going to talk in here. I'll shut your office door when we're done."

"Sure, brother. And Claire, it's good to see you."

She gave a slight nod, looking shyer than ever. He wanted to take her worry and doubt and toss it all away. Zeke left, and whatever connection they'd gained out in the main room of the bar seemed to have evaporated in the smaller confines of the office.

"Hey," she finally said, her voice soft.

He reached up and cupped her face now. "Hey."

Her gaze stayed on his. He took that as a good sign. He leaned in, hesitating to give her time to say no. But she didn't tell him to stop. Instead, she closed the distance. Their lips met in a sweet slide that made him wonder if he was dreaming.

His throat closed like he had eaten something too sweet for words, then his heart started racing. He would push them too fast, and he didn't want that. She had been through too much for him to push. He took a step back and swallowed over the lust pumping through him.

"I…I'm not sure why you're here or what to say." He sounded stupid. But he'd never been in a situation like this before.

"I don't know, but you're the only person I could think of when I figured out…"

He reached out, his hand landing on her shoulder. "Figured what out?"

Tears were back in her eyes, and it felt like someone had punched him. He pulled her close, wanting to help her more than anything else he'd ever wanted.

"Tell me everything."

Claire took a step away and shook her head. For a moment, he thought she wouldn't speak. A lump formed in his chest and made it hard to breathe. He wanted to tell her she was safe, but maybe she wasn't. What had happened once she left Fallport?

"My dad forged my name."

Her words didn't make sense at first. Then she turned to him, and he could tell this was ripping her apart. He needed more information.

Eric stilled, anger rose, and he didn't want her to think he was mad at her, so he spoke as plainly as he could, but he probably failed. "How bad is it?"

"Everything. Like he forged my name on documents when I was a teenager implicating me as the one who wanted to start laundering money and embezzling. I have documents, you know, the financial stuff, but I don't know what to do to prove I wasn't a part of his scheming."

Eric closed his eyes, wondering if he knew anyone who could help. His friends were mostly blue-collar types, maybe a few artisans. Smart in their own right, but not people who could wade through financial documents.

The door opened, and Zeke stepped in. "Dang it. I forgot you two were in here." Zeke's eyes narrowed. "Is everything okay?"

Eric shook his head. "Tell Zeke. Maybe he can help."

Claire drew in a ragged breath. "I don't know what to do. My dad made it look like I was the one who wanted to do all the financial crimes."

Zeke's lips pressed together. "You need to talk to Drew."

Eric cocked his head to the side, then it hit him. "Of course, Drew. He might be able to help you work out what happened."

"Who is Drew?"

"He's a great guy. Used to be a cop, then he became an accountant. He likes working with numbers. He's a great guy, and maybe he can get you in touch with someone who can help, you know, since he knows finances and used to be a cop," Zeke said.

For the first time since Claire returned, she seemed hopeful. Her eyes were brighter, and the frown lines crisscrossing her forehead were smoothed out.

"Oh gosh, that would be amazing."

Zeke picked up something from his desk. "I just came in to grab this. You two take as much time as you need. I'll tell you if Drew comes in." Zeke pulled his phone from his pocket. "I'm going to text him and see if he's free."

"Thank you," Claire said as Zeke slipped out. "I can't believe I found someone willing to help."

"I'm glad. I—um, where are you staying?"

Her gaze met his, then slowly slid away. "I don't know. I guess I could—"

Before she could say more, he interrupted. "Stay with me."

Her gaze shot to his, and her eyes went wide. He needed to explain.

"I mean, you don't have to sleep with me. I have a guest room. I just want to make sure you're safe."

"Is that all?"

He swallowed over his internal doubts. Maybe he wasn't enough for Claire, or maybe she wasn't really interested, but the few kisses they'd shared had turned him inside out.

"I don't want to push you into something you don't want, but I'm interested in you. I don't know your plans, but if we had a chance, maybe something would grow."

Claire didn't move or say anything, and he wondered if he'd gone too far. He wasn't anything special, and maybe she wanted more from life than to be stuck in a town like Fallport with someone like him.

CHAPTER TWENTY-TWO

Claire couldn't believe her luck. She'd come here expecting a reprieve but hadn't thought she'd find help.

"Thank you." She moved closer. "No, really, thank you. I mean it. I didn't know where else to go. I just left."

"Are you okay?"

She blew out a breath filled with frustration. "Yes. I mean, I'm upset and took the overnight train, so I didn't sleep well, and I'm exhausted, but I'm okay."

"Do your parents know where you are?"

"No. I left and wrote a note, telling them I was leaving and not to look for me."

"What happened?"

"I went back and started thinking. I couldn't sleep so I went to the office and found everything. I found all the documentation. My dad used me. He set me up for failure. I felt so totally alone, and all I could think of was Fallport…" she trailed off, not wanting to reveal how desperate she was for him.

He studied her face, his gaze filled with caring. She couldn't hide from him. He was too important. Maybe she was jumping the gun trusting him like this, but she felt deep in her soul he wouldn't turn on her like her family had.

"I thought of you, too."

He rested his forehead against hers. "You feel it, too?"

She nodded and reached out, placing her hand on his waist. "I do. I feel so much for you, and it's weird."

"Why weird?"

"Because we don't know each other."

He moved just a little, enough to kiss her cheek. "We know a lot for how little time we've spent together."

No question, Eric got that right. They did know a lot about each other for the limited time they'd had.

"I'm glad I found you that morning in the diner. I feel like that morning made everything else possible."

"I would have wanted to save you no matter what, but I'm not sure we would have trusted each other if we hadn't eaten together that morning."

"I do trust you."

"Good, because I only have your best interest at heart."

She took a step back, knowing that she needed to resolve a few things before she got into a relationship with Eric. He didn't need her past coming back to bite him in the rear. If her father was ever investigated, she'd end up in prison.

"First, I need to solve this issue with my family. I can't have this…" She searched for a word, not sure exactly what to call it.

"The mess your father put you in?" Eric asked.

She rolled her eyes. "Yeah, I can't have his crap hanging over your head."

"I don't feel like it is. I think we can get it solved."

"I just don't want you to suffer."

He pulled her into a hug, and she was careful not to touch his injured arm. It felt good to hold him. This was what she'd been missing her whole life.

The door opened, and this time it wasn't Zeke. It was a man she'd never met before. Eric stepped back, and a smile broke out over his face.

"Just the man we need to see." Eric reached out and shook the other man's hand. "Drew, this is Claire. She needs help."

Drew smiled and moved to her, reaching out to shake her hand. Her stomach tumbled as she took his hand, fear almost overwhelming her. What if this man couldn't help her, and she ended up in prison, anyway?

"I'm Drew. I don't know exactly what's up, but Zeke said I should talk to you." Drew pointed to the two chairs and nodded. "Let's sit, and you can explain what happened."

Claire worried that telling anyone else would put

her in more danger. But how much more danger could she experience than being taken hostage, shot at, and chased down a mountain? Maybe Drew could really help her.

She took a deep breath and explained the situation with her father laundering money. She told Drew how he'd been using her as an accomplice without her knowledge, how she'd stumbled upon evidence of his activities, and now she was afraid that if the authorities found out, she could end up in prison even if she hadn't known what he was doing.

Drew listened patiently, his expression growing more serious the more she spoke. He asked questions as she talked and took a few notes. When she finished, he was quiet for a long moment. Desperation began to fill her. She was helpless against the schemes of her father. Maybe she could just leave and live a quiet life out west. Maybe she could escape him if no one ever knew who she was.

Drew tapped the files she'd pulled out. "This will be tough, but I think I can help you." Drew leaned forward and held her gaze. "It won't be easy, and there is still a chance you may end up in some trouble depending on how things play out. We'll have to take it one step at a time."

Claire sighed, finally feeling some hope return. "Do you really think I could get out from under some of this?"

"It depends on what your father does. Are you staying in Fallport?"

She nodded. "I'm staying with Eric."

"Good. That will give me some time to talk to a few people." He turned to Eric. "How are you doing?"

"I'm okay."

Drew nodded and turned back to her. "The people who abducted you. They were pissed at your father. They could try to act again. Both of you need to be careful. Drew, you have an alarm on your place, right?"

He nodded. "I do."

That made Claire feel a little better. She had no idea who or what would come after her. Maybe her father would change his business strategy, and nothing would happen to her, but they had to be prepared.

"Thank you for your help in this matter," Eric said.

"I've spent my life following the law. I know accounting may not seem like it's the same as police work, but making sure people understand the ramifications of lying in their financial books is part of being an accountant. I'm glad you came to me with this. I think we can clear a few things up and keep you out of trouble."

"Thank you. I'll forever be in your debt," Claire said.

Drew shook his head. "Naw, I'm happy to help." Drew stood and shook her hand after she stood, too. "I'll be in touch. And stay safe."

"Thank you," she said again as Drew left the office.

She breathed out a sigh of relief. She'd been so

upset when she'd figured out her father had used her. Now there might be a light at the end of the tunnel.

"You ready to go?" Eric asked.

She nodded. "I just need to grab my suitcase, and we can head out."

Claire finally felt like she could get out from under this. Maybe her father would fight her, but she could turn this around. She had no idea what to do here in Fallport, but at least she had options. It made sense why her father had wanted her close. Now she wondered if they'd ever cared for her.

She glanced over at Eric, smiling when he smiled. This man cared. That much was obvious. She just hoped her family didn't retaliate. Because if they did, this time, she might not survive.

CHAPTER TWENTY-THREE

Again the awkward feeling hit Claire as she entered Eric's home. She knew he wanted her here, but her past seemed to be creeping up on her. The weirdness also seemed to have hit Eric, as he seemed unsure what to do. Why were they so awkward together?

"I'll show you to the guest room," Eric said.

She nodded, knowing that sleeping in his bed would be weird. The thought of being with him sent heat through her. Maybe she should have stayed at a hotel.

"The shower is right across the hall. I'll heat up some dinner. Then we can…I don't know, talk maybe?"

She blew out a breath as frustration filled her. "Why are we so awkward together?" Her eyes went wide as embarrassment hit. "Oh God, I didn't mean to say that out loud. I just—" Heat washed up her face, and she turned from him, trying to hide.

JULIA BRIGHT

His hand on her arm was firm, and he pushed at her shoulder. After another push, she turned to face him, peeking out from behind her hands.

"I'm sorry. I shouldn't have said that. I—"

"Don't apologize. I feel it, too. And I don't know. We shared a lot."

She nodded. "We did." She stepped closer to him and reached out, putting her hand on his chest. Her gaze darted to his lips. "I know I'm not ready to jump into bed with you, but—" She looked up, meeting his gaze, and swallowed. "I have feelings."

He nodded. "I do, too."

"Maybe we should explore those feelings and see what happens."

"I think I know what will happen," Eric said.

Confusion hit Claire. "What?"

Eric chuckled before he leaned in and brushed his lips over hers. She gasped, and her mouth opened. He took the opportunity and swiped his tongue against hers, bringing forth a raw moan. Her core flexed as excitement twisted through her. She wanted more but didn't want to hurt him.

She took a step back and glanced up at him. "Your arm?"

"My arm has nothing to do with what I'm feeling." Eric pressed in, grazing his hips against hers. She felt the swell of his hard length and gasped.

"Oh."

"I won't pressure you but know that I want you."

More heat washed over her. "I'm not a virgin, but I'm not experienced."

"We don't have to do anything. But I don't want you thinking I'm not interested."

Claire's hands shook as she ran them over his chest, wondering how far she was willing to go. She pulled up the hem of his shirt and slid her fingers over his hot skin. She moved them across his hip and then toward his belly. He moaned, encouraging her. She loved the feel of the fuzz on his belly just above the waistband of his jeans.

He moaned again and rocked his hips. Her gaze slammed into his. The need in his eyes ramped up her anticipation. She squeezed her legs together, trying to get her desire under control. It didn't help.

Eric reached up and pulled off his shirt, only wincing a little. She stared at him, admiring his toned muscles. His tanned skin seemed to almost glow with a warmth that called to her. She wanted to be naked and up against him. She wondered what her creamy breasts would look like pressed against his pecs.

Claire was just about to remove her shirt when the doorbell pealed, interrupting them.

Eric's nostrils flared, and he shook his head. "Dang it." He grabbed his shirt and pulled it on, growling as he left the room.

Claire stood in the bedroom, trying to calm her breath, when she heard someone speaking. She moved to the hall so she could see Drew standing in the entry-way. When his gaze hit hers, he frowned.

"We have a problem," Drew said.

Panic raced through her, and she reached up, clutching her throat. She hated that her father had put her in this situation. This would ruin her life, and it could destroy Eric's life, too. That was the last thing she wanted. Maybe she should leave.

"What is the problem?" Eric asked.

"I did some searching. It's more than just a few documents. Her father opened accounts in her name. Just based on the reports I ran, if anyone in law enforcement even took one look at this mess, you'd end up in jail for a long time."

Panic hit, and she gasped. She had no idea her father had done something to make her life such hell. What was she going to do? Drew and Eric both looked at her, their faces filled with concern.

"What can I do?" Claire asked, tears filling her eyes. She was overwhelmed by the situation and wasn't sure what to do next. She could end up in real trouble, and her father hadn't cared.

Drew glanced at Eric before turning back to her. "I know someone in the FBI who might be able to help," he said. "We could talk to him and see if he has any ideas."

"Do you think that would work?" Claire asked.

Drew shrugged. "It's your best bet. If you go to the authorities, you'll have a better chance of getting out from under this. If you just let things progress without talking to authorities, you might end up paying with your life spent in prison."

Fear filled her. "I don't want that."

"I understand," Drew said. "Let me call my friend, and I'll get back to you. You might need to go to DC or another city to get this all sorted out."

She closed her eyes and shook her head. "How could he have done this to me?"

Eric put his arm around her shoulder and pulled her close. "We'll figure this out."

She glanced up, regret and anger filling her. "I'm so sorry. I didn't mean to drag you into this."

Eric cupped her face. "Hey, you didn't drag me into anything. I want to help you. We'll figure this out together."

She stepped into his embrace and rested her head on his chest. She didn't know if they would make it through this, but at least with Eric standing beside her, she wouldn't be alone.

CHAPTER TWENTY-FOUR

Claire hadn't slept well though the bed at Eric's place was comfortable. The room wasn't stuffy either. She liked being here but worry ate at her. She'd woken early, found coffee, and headed to the screened-in back patio.

She sipped her coffee, trying not to freak out about her problems, but it was difficult. Eric opened the door and stuck his head out.

"Good morning." The warmth in Eric's voice wrapped around her, giving her comfort.

Her smile came naturally, and she realized that even though she hadn't slept well, she felt great because she was here with this man. "Hey, how are you this morning?"

Eric rolled his shoulder and slowly stretched his arm. "I'm going to need to spend time stretching my arm to get back my mobility, but it's not bad. The infection is gone, or it feels like it's gone. I don't feel off anymore. Like my head is clear now, not like it was for the last few days."

She was glad to hear he was doing better. "That's great."

"How are you doing this morning?"

Eric's question hit hard. She didn't know how she was doing. Confusion swirled, and she worried she was making too much of what she'd found. She shrugged and went back to staring out at the backyard. "I'm glad I found the coffee."

Eric chuckled. "Speaking of that, I'm going to grab a mug. Do you need anything else?"

She shook her head. "No thank you. I'm fine."

He stepped back into the house, and she wondered if she was fine. So much had happened, and she worried that it would never end. She was so lost in her thoughts that she didn't notice Eric returning until he slid into the seat next to her. Thankfully, she didn't jump.

She nodded at his yard. "It's nice out here. Peaceful. I love the flowers."

Eric had multiple beds of flowers and pots with flowers. She had never lived anywhere she could garden, so she had no idea why some flowers were in pots. But the area looked amazing.

"Thanks. My grandmother loved flowers. She always had a great garden and loved to sit and watch the sunrise. You can't see the sunrise from my yard because of the positioning of the house, but I feel like I've honored her memory with this garden."

Claire smiled as her heart warmed for him. "That's so sweet."

"Did your family plant flowers?"

She shook her head and then took another sip from her mug. "Never. We never lived in a house with a good yard. If we had a yard, it was mostly dead grass. No one cared about making it look good."

Eric set down his coffee. "That's kind of sad. This yard helps keep me centered."

"I like it. I swear, before I came out here this morning, there was a big animal in the yard. At least I thought I saw it when I looked out the window, but now I doubt what I saw."

Eric lifted his eyebrows as he sipped his coffee, giving her a questioning look. He lowered his mug and responded. "You know, it was probably a deer. There are a few that come into town."

She wasn't sure she'd ever seen a deer in the wild. Her life in both California and Baltimore had been lived in the city. "Wow, that's awesome."

Eric chuckled. "They are kind of seen as pests. I mean, I know people think they are cute, but they eat everything and dig up flowers, and do other stuff to mess up the yard. The males can be aggressive, and when they have their antlers, those things can be dangerous. I get that they seem so sweet, but sometimes they are jerks. So never approach them."

Claire laughed. It felt good to be here with Eric. Her worries felt so far away. "That's good advice. I'll remember never to play with the deer."

They were silent for a moment as they sipped their coffee and watched the birds flit through the yard. After a moment, Drew leaned in and pointed to a blue flower. "I like the hydrangeas, the blue ones."

She stared at the very blue flowers. "They almost look unnatural. How did they get so blue?"

"I put down some aluminum sulfate which adds acid and turns them blue. They were my grandmother's fav—"

Just then, Eric's phone went off, interrupting them. He met her gaze, and worry blasted through her. She held her breath as he answered the phone.

"Hello, Drew."

She prayed nothing bad was going down. She needed something good to happen. So much had gone wrong in the last few days. She wasn't sure how she would recover.

"Let me put you on speaker." Eric set his phone down on the arm of his chair and then clicked the dot to activate the speaker phone.

Claire slowed her breathing because she was almost at panic level. This could change everything.

"Hello, Claire. I was telling Eric that my contact at the FBI wants to talk to you. He said he wants to do a video call this afternoon at one. Is that okay?"

She swallowed over the rising fear. "Y-yes."

"Don't worry. He's a good guy. His name is Noah Grey. He's been an agent for a while. I've known him for years. He was in Texas and then moved to Virginia. That's how I know him. He was very concerned when I told him about your family implicating you when you were a child. He said that's going to work in your favor."

She reached for her mug, but her hands were shaking so she clenched them in her lap instead of clutching her coffee. "I really appreciate any help. I don't know what to do. And I'm afraid of what would happen to me if anyone ever investigated."

"We'll make sure you aren't taken advantage of," Drew said.

"Thank you." Those two words didn't express how she felt, but she was at a loss for what else to say. This could save her. She felt almost overwhelmed by the offer to help. She'd really thought she would have to run away and live off the grid.

"I'll be over a little before one, Eric," Drew said.

"Oh, you're going to be with us, too?" Claire asked.

"I'm not going to leave you hanging. I trust Noah, but I know you aren't an accountant. I'll be there to make sure you understand what's happening."

Claire breathed out a huge sigh, and tears filled her eyes. Eric picked up the phone and stepped inside, leaving her on the patio. She wiped at her eyes, wishing she wasn't so emotional. It seemed like everything was making her cry. But this was good, and yet tears still leaked from her eyes.

After a moment, Eric stepped outside again. "Hey, how about some breakfast? Then we can go for a short walk before we shower and get dressed."

She swiped at her eyes again, trying to erase the evidence of her overactive emotions, and nodded. "Sounds good. I'm hungry."

"That's good. I have some bacon and eggs along with toast."

"I like breakfast food."

Claire stepped inside, taking in the kitchen. Though she didn't know where anything was, she wanted to help, so she searched for the plates and silverware while Eric cooked. She poured more coffee for both of them and set it on the table just as Eric finished cooking. The food smelled amazing, and she was ready to dig in.

Being here felt comfortable. Maybe more comfortable than she'd ever felt with her family. Claire took a bite and smiled as flavors burst on her tongue. "This is really delicious." She took another bite and moaned.

"Thank you. I can cook a mean breakfast. I also do well with fish and burgers. I've learned to cook fairly well since I'm on my own."

Claire glanced at her plate and lifted her head just enough to see Eric. "Were you always on your own?" Claire shook her head, worry twisting through her. "Sorry, I don't need to pry. Don't answer that."

Eric chuckled. "I've never been married. I'm older than you are, so I've had a few serious girlfriends. One I thought would be the one, but she didn't want me leaving the Marines and sure as heck didn't want to live here in Fallport. Turns out, she was cheating on me. She liked me being deployed so she could go off and shag other guys."

"Ouch," Claire said. "I'm sorry she did that. Honestly, I feel like you should never cheat. If you're going to be with someone else, tell the person you're with. That way, they have a fair chance."

Eric lifted his eyebrows. "A fair chance to do what?"

She shrugged. "I don't know. I just couldn't go behind someone's back. I think that's what hurts so much about my dad doing this thing with the money. Not that it's the same as a relationship, but he went behind my back and stabbed me. I've always thought that being open and forthcoming with relationships was best. Like if I don't like something, I'm going to speak up."

"And if you do like something?" Eric asked.

Heat filled her face, and she glanced down, breaking eye contact. "That's harder to ask for."

"I like you a lot."

Her head whipped up, and now the heat inside was like a volcano. Could she tell him that she wanted him? Her body certainly responded to him, and she thought he was a good guy. He was everything good, and she needed someone like him to make her life better. "I like you, too. I guess I should be open and honest about that. I want to be in your bed soon, not just to sleep."

Eric's lips spread into a wide grin, and he picked up a forkful of food, stuffing it into his mouth. Neither one of them spoke as they finished their meal, but they both shot glances each other's way. Now they were seriously flirting, and it felt good.

"How about that walk?" Eric asked after he finished his breakfast.

"Sure, sounds good."

They washed the dishes and wiped down the table before Claire headed to the bathroom to freshen up. She met Eric at the front door a few minutes later. Shyness had seeped in, but she remembered what she'd said at the table and moved close enough to go up on her toes and kiss his cheek.

He smiled and took her hand, leading her outside. They walked along the road, enjoying being together. She pointed out flowers and trees she thought looked good. He told her what they were. After a few minutes, Claire began talking about how her family moved around so much when she was younger. She hated losing friends when they moved, but that's how it worked with her family.

"That must have been hard," Eric said.

Claire sighed. "Yeah, it was. I mean, I didn't always hate moving because it meant a new location. I hated Oklahoma because of all the tornados. The house behind us was destroyed by one, and the whole family died."

"Oh, that's awful."

"Yeah. It easily could have been us. I was terrified. I think my mom hated it, too. We moved shortly after that family died."

"Where did you move to?"

"Crowded California. Los Angeles. We were smack dab in the middle of the city with millions of people around us."

"Oh, ouch. I lived in San Diego for a few years. It wasn't my favorite place where I was stationed."

"Where was your favorite place?"

"Honestly, in Japan. Here in the States, I think Virginia. It's not too hot and not too cold for too long on the coast."

"I've never even thought about going into the military."

Eric chuckled. "Trust me, don't."

"It was that bad?"

He shook his head. "Not for me. But I knew guys and women who didn't want to be in the military but felt they had no choice. They hated every minute. If you don't want to go in, don't. It's not a cure-all. I liked it to a point, but there's a reason I'm not in the military any longer. I could have stayed in for my twenty-five and been retired in about fifteen years. It wasn't worth it for me."

"How was your life growing up?" Claire asked. "Was there a reason you wanted to join the military?"

"My parents were great. They encouraged me when I expressed an interest in woodwork. Said they wanted me to thrive. Then, when I was fifteen, my dad died. It was hard on me."

"Wow, that sounds tough."

"It was. The worst was my mom had to work two jobs for money. Even then, she had trouble making the bills. Seeing her struggle probably had more to do with me joining the military than anything else." Eric quieted as they rounded the corner.

She glanced at him and noticed worry lines on his forehead and that his mouth was down in a frown. She wanted to say something but didn't know what. It sounded like he'd had some tough times as a kid.

"It wasn't all bad, joining up and all. I wanted to make a difference for my mom, so while I was in high school, I worked really hard and did dual enrollment classes. When I graduated high school, I needed two classes to get an associate's degree. That got me more money in the military. I was able to send most of it home to my mom. She appreciated it so much that she went to school and got a better job. She wanted to pay me back. I told her no, but she sent the money to me anyway."

"Wow, that's some story." Hearing how Eric and his mother had done so much for each other was wild. Her dad had used her, potentially destroying her life, and

Eric's mother had worked hard to get ahead just to help Eric.

Eric chuckled. "I took that money and have it in a fund to help her if she needs assistance when she's older. I don't think she'll need it, though. She moved to California for the job she got after graduation, and she met a really nice guy. They got married. Most of all, she's happy, and I'm thrilled for her."

Claire couldn't help but smile. "That's awesome." She wondered how different her life would have been if her family wanted the best for her like Eric's parents had wanted for him.

Would anything in her life have been different? She was still young and could change things. Nothing was set in stone. Heck, even if she got older, her life wouldn't be set in stone. Unless she went to prison for her father's crimes. Then everything would be bad.

A groan escaped her lips, and Eric put his hand on her shoulder. "What is it?"

"Nothing, everything. I should have stayed in college." Depression wove through her.

"You know, you could always go back."

She nodded. "I just don't know how anything will play out. And I won't have money, and stuff will be hard. Maybe I'll do something else. I can always just play music. Like, I don't need a degree for that. It just all seems so daunting."

Eric squeezed her shoulder, giving her comfort. "You have time to decide."

She nodded, realizing they'd gone full circle, and were back at his house.

"I guess we need to get ready for Drew and Noah now," Claire said.

"We should. You can shower first, then I'll shower."

Heat crept up her cheeks. She wanted to say they could shower together, but Drew was coming over, and she needed to be prepared for her meeting with Noah. Drew's friend may be nice, but the FBI was still the police, and they may not believe her.

CHAPTER TWENTY-FIVE

The phone call with Noah was enlightening. Before they ended the call, Noah clasped his hands in front of himself on the desk and leaned in.

"Claire, the information you've given the FBI will help to clear your name. There's no way you, as a thirteen-year-old, could have devised a plan to launder money that was as sophisticated as this. I know teenagers are smart, but with everything you've told me and what I've seen, there is evidence you were taken advantage of. What your family did could have ruined you for life. If the wrong authorities got this information without you coming forward and telling your side first, I think the chances are you would have spent years in prison."

She swallowed over the lump forming in her throat. She didn't want to think about how bad it could have gone. Her family had screwed her over.

"Do you think my mom knew, too?"

Noah sighed. "It will take a deeper investigation before we know for sure. I'll talk to my superiors and tell them what you told me. They'll have questions, and I'm sure you'll have to come out and talk with them, but the files on the drive, along with the paper copies you took, really helped us."

"Thank you."

"No, ma'am, thank you. Coming forward takes bravery. Other people know about their families' crimes and never tell us. I'm glad you had the courage to speak up. I'll be in contact with you later. Drew tells me you're in Fallport and that you have a place to stay. That's a nice town. Relax and enjoy your time there. It may take a while to get to this, so if I don't call in the next few days, don't think we're ignoring it. There are just a lot of things that have to happen."

"Sure. I won't worry, and I will enjoy the town."

"Good. It was great meeting you. Bye."

The call ended, and Claire sat back, blowing out a breath. A twinge of fear slid through her. What if she'd screwed up? What if what she'd found wasn't as bad as she thought?

"Hey, Claire, you did the right thing," Eric said softly.

She nodded but couldn't hold back the tears. He pulled her close, and she clung to him, sobbing against his chest. It took a long moment for her to calm down.

Drew had made her tea and brought over a plate of cookies.

She grabbed a cookie and took a bite, staring at the table as she chewed. "What if my parents are innocent?"

Drew cleared his throat. "Based on what I saw, there is no way your parents innocently placed the blame for their criminal activity on you. They knew you were too young to say or do anything. They hid the truth from you, and honestly, I think it's why your parents forced you to quit college and go home."

She narrowed her gaze and then turned to Eric. "Did you tell him that?"

Drew held up both hands. "Hold on. He didn't tell me anything private, only that your parents had forced you to quit school."

She nodded. "They did. I just...I feel guilty turning them in. I was just so mad when I found out what they did. I was almost killed because of my father's illegal activity, and then I found out he'd made it look like I was the guilty one in our family. He did so much bad stuff under my name."

"It was absolutely wrong what he did," Eric said. "I want to make sure you know you have a place here. You're safe here."

"Fallport is a small town, which means there will be loads of people watching out for you," Drew smirked. "There're loads of gossip, so people will know about some of this stuff, but those gossips will look out for you."

Claire cringed. "Gossips? How many people will know?"

"A lot," Eric said. "They still talk about my ex leaving me. But they also are protective of me. They want me to succeed. It's weird when you're not used to it, but the people here are good overall."

She shook her head. "I'm sure I'll get used to it."

"Good. And if you need anything, don't hesitate to call," Drew said.

"Thank you,"

"No problem. Both of you, get some rest, and I'll see you around town."

Eric walked Drew out and came back in a moment later. She'd washed her mug and cleaned up the cookies. When she turned around to face Eric, a lump formed in her throat.

She'd been through so much, but all she could think about was holding him. She wanted to pull him to the couch and make out until they both fell asleep.

"What are you thinking?" Eric asked.

She let go a heavy sigh. "Based on our conversation earlier, I'm just going to be honest with you."

"Okay," Eric said slowly like he was suspicious of her motives.

"I want to strip off my clothes, get in your bed, and see what happens."

"Oh. That's not what I expected, but I'm all for that."

Laughter bubbled up, and she moved to him, a wide smile on her lips. "So you wouldn't mind getting naked with me?"

He shook his head. "Not at all. I'd love to strip off my clothes and be naked with you."

She pulled at his shirt, and he helped her, tossing it on the back of the kitchen chair. Then he kicked off his shoes and unbuttoned his jeans. She stepped back and watched, appreciating the show.

"You're very sexy."

His chuckle warmed her. "So are you. Now then," he said as he stepped closer to her, only wearing his socks and underwear. "How about we see what happens when you take off your clothes?"

She ran her hand down his torso, pausing just above his belly button. "Do you like getting your cock sucked?"

He nodded as he pulled her shirt up. "I do. What about you? Do you like getting licked until you scream?"

A shiver took over, and her whole body shook. "So I'm not a virgin, but I'm inexperienced. No one has ever done that."

He took a step back. "So no guy has ever gone down on you?"

She shook her head as embarrassment filled her. "No. I mean, guys have grabbed my breasts, and I was with one guy. We did it twice, but it wasn't anything really special. It's why I never have…well, I just don't think sex is that great. I like kissing."

"Oh, honey, I'm going to make sure you have a good time." He took her hand and led her to his room. They were beside his bed, kissing as Eric continued to remove her clothes.

Once she was naked, he pushed her to the mattress and then slowly kissed his way up her thigh to her hip. It took a few licks and nibbles before he spread her legs and then kissed his way over to her center. When his mouth covered her pussy, she jumped.

Eric slid his hands up her belly, pressing her back. His tongue licked over her center, then plunged inside her before he sucked down on her clit. The sucking and licking was driving her crazy. Her toes curled, and her feet were pointed so hard she thought she would get a cramp in her feet or legs.

Then Eric sucked her in one more time, and she almost screamed. Whatever he was doing felt so good. Her whole body vibrated. She didn't know if she could hold it together. She screamed his name, half thinking she should beg him to stop.

She couldn't breathe or think or speak, and she thought she would burst into a million pieces. But then the most wonderful feeling took over. It was like something miraculous overcame her.

The feeling was so overwhelming she couldn't keep her eyes open or even think. Her brain seemed to blank, and she might have passed out for a second.

When she opened her eyes, Eric was above her, staring at her with something like reverence. She reached up, touching his cheek.

"What was that?"

He moved to stretch out beside her. "That's what sex is supposed to be like."

"What?" She moved to sit up, but he pressed her back to the mattress. "That's what's supposed to happen? I thought that was all a myth."

"Well, now you've experienced it and know it's not a myth."

"Damn, that was amazing."

"I'm glad you liked it."

She rolled to her side. "But what about you?"

"I'm fine for now. We can do more later."

"But—"

His lips covered hers, and she opened for him. When the kiss ended, he pulled back. "You were so excited when you came that it pushed me over the edge."

"Oh. Does that happen?"

"Not often. Actually, never. I was just so wrapped up in you it felt good to give you something so amazing. You were very enthusiastic, and it made me so hot."

Her face heated. "I'm a little embarrassed."

"Trust me, don't be. That was freaking amazing. If our next experience is half as good, I will be happy. I mean, you shouting my name like that. It was an ego boost."

Laughter bubbled up, and she moved to cuddle close to him. She liked how he'd made her feel. Their activities left her wondering what else she'd never experienced. She had a lot to learn and was glad Eric would be the teacher.

CHAPTER TWENTY-SIX

Eric hadn't planned on falling asleep, but he woke to find Claire pressed against him. His cock was nestled against her ass, and it felt so good. She moaned and reached back, pulling him closer.

"Don't pull away," Claire moaned.

He moved his hand and found it was draped over her, close to her breast. She felt so good up against him, her ass pressing against his hard cock, driving lust through his veins. He slowly slid his hand over and cupped her breast, his thumb grazing over her nipple. She hissed in a breath and pushed back, grinding against his cock.

He moaned and moved his lips so they were on her neck. He wanted more. He was about to say something when she reached back and grasped his cock.

He sucked in a breath as lust pumped harder. Her hand on him felt so good that he just went with her move. He hadn't realized that she was positioning him to slide in until his cockhead was at her entrance.

"Are you sure?" Eric asked.

"Yes. I want you."

He pushed his hips forward, sliding slowly into her. She was tight and hot and so wet he felt like he was in heaven. She wiggled a little, and that pushed him in deeper. He moaned, and she froze.

"Was that okay?"

"Oh yeah. You feel so good. So freaking good."

Her chuckle vibrated through her, and he thought he would lose it. The feeling of being deep inside had turned him inside out. He clung to her as he filled her with his cock.

"Fuck, too good," Eric moaned.

She pushed back against him, and he had to respond. He grasped her hips and pulled her tight against him until his cock was buried so deep that he saw stars. Based on how she was moaning and grinding her ass against him, she wanted this as much as he did.

His balls were ready to blow again, and his heart raced as he pulled out and snapped his hips forward. He tried to hold back, to make this a slow and steady lovemaking session, but the way she was moving against him drove him crazy.

He adjusted a little and reached between her legs, finding her swollen clit. She was just as turned on as he was.

"More," Claire groaned.

He wanted to bring her pleasure and make her feel more. They were molten fire together. They were both breathing heavily, and he knew he wouldn't last.

Claire arched her back, sticking her ass out, making him slide in deeper. When she squirmed again, it was all he could do to keep from coming.

Her orgasm hit, and that drove him over the edge. He shoved in and pumped his cum into her, wondering only after he was finished if she was on birth control. He would ask later. He should have thought about it before.

It was weird how different he felt with Claire. She made him feel things he didn't think were accessible to him any longer. She had changed his outlook on so many things.

He was naturally positive, but he thought he would never find anyone to be his partner. But here he was, ready to create a life with Claire. That kind of scared him. But losing her frightened him more.

"How was that for you?" Eric asked.

"So good. I guess we need to get up and fix dinner."

He nodded. "Yeah, I am hungry."

Slowly, they pulled on their clothes, exchanging looks and smiling at each other. Eric had a warmth inside he hadn't ever felt. Being with her changed things. He could see a future with this woman.

The smiling at each other continued as they heated leftovers in the microwave. Before they moved to sit down, he pulled her close and kissed her like he meant it. After eating, they took another leisurely walk around town, talking more about the trees and flowers. Claire seemed hungry to know more about the natural flora and fauna.

That night, she made it clear she was sleeping with him. As he lay with her in his arms, her body soft against his, he knew true contentment. The steady beat of her heart and her soft breath puffing against his skin made his throat close with emotions. He had never felt this way about anyone and wanted to make sure they stayed together.

In the morning, a smile spread across his face as he opened his eyes to see Claire sleeping beside him. Soft rays of morning light spilled into the room, illuminating Claire's beautiful face. Her eyes feathered open, and she reached out, running her hand down his chest, past his belly button, and lower to his hard cock.

She pushed his shoulder to the mattress, then rose and straddled him, sliding slowly down his cock. The wet heat felt so good he closed his eyes as she moved above him. The need to see her rose, and he flashed them open, drinking in the sight of her full breasts and beautiful face.

This was perfection. He would fight for this woman. She brought out an instinct so primal it hurt. He would keep her safe and treasure her because Claire was the real deal.

After a quick shower, they headed out to get coffee at Grinders. The coffee shop was a local meeting place, but this morning it was empty when they stepped in. One of his favorite baristas was back in town.

"Hey, April, how are you doing?" April smiled and waved. She and Mac had come back to Fallport after finishing their university degrees.

"Hi, Eric! It's great to see you. I was wondering how you were doing after the shooting."

"I'm healing. How's Mac?"

"He's great. He got the job with the forestry service. He starts in two months. We probably won't be in Fallport for long, but we'll be back to visit my aunt."

"That's great news. It's good to hear you both got what you wanted. I'm happy for you. This is Claire," Eric said as he put his arm around her.

"Hi," Claire flashed a smile. "Do you know where you will be moving?"

April shook her head. "No, but we're both happy to go wherever we are sent. I know not everyone is prepared to move across the country for a job, but I'm happy to go with him."

"That's good."

"So, Claire, how long are you here in Fallport?"

She shrugged. "I don't know. I'd like to stay for a while. I like this area. Things are just…" Claire glanced behind them, and I saw Otto stepping in.

"We should order, and we can talk later."

April's lips tipped up, and she nodded. "Hey, Otto, I'll get to your order in a moment."

"Same as usual." Otto zeroed in on Claire. "Who are you?"

He felt Claire stiffen and suddenly wanted to protect her. He was about to open his mouth and say something when Claire smiled sweetly and moved to Otto.

"Hello, I'm Claire. And you're Otto. So what do you like most about Fallport?"

"Are you some kind of reporter? You're pretty enough, but you don't have a camera."

Claire leaned in, her eyes going wide. "Are you sure I don't have a secret camera?"

Otto narrowed his eyes and then laughed. "You're funny." Otto turned to Eric and pointed at Claire. "You should keep this one. She's funny, unlike that other lady you used to date. She was mean. This one is pretty, too. Don't fuck this up, boy."

Claire smiled and patted Otto on the shoulder. "Stop, you're going to give me a complex. I'm not funny."

"Sure you are, sweetie. Tell me, are you living with him? You should know he spends way too much time with wood."

Eric lost what Claire and Otto were talking about as he finished placing their order for coffee. He didn't dislike Otto, but the man spread gossip faster than butter melted over hot corn. When he stepped over to the table where Otto was sitting, the older man hit him with a serious look.

"Your girlfriend just told me she was the woman abducted in the forest last week. You need to keep her safe. I've got a bad feeling about that." Otto turned to Claire. "Sorry, ma'am, but I don't trust your parents. I heard them talking. Didn't say nothing, but I don't trust them."

Eric nodded, understanding the concern. He agreed with Otto that Claire needed more security, but he knew her family didn't know where she was, so he kept his thoughts to himself.

"Nice seeing you, Otto." Eric held out his hand to Claire. "You ready?"

"Sure."

"Nice to meet you, young lady," Otto said.

Claire patted him on his back before turning and following Eric outside and across the street to the square. They headed to the gazebo and settled, looking out onto the park.

Eric sipped his coffee as he watched Claire take in her surroundings with a hint of apprehension.

"What's wrong?" Eric asked softly as he reached out to take her hand.

Claire sighed heavily and turned to look at him, her eyes full of worry. "It's just...I mean...do you really think there's a need for me to have more security? I mean, it's not like my parents know where I am or anything..." She trailed off, biting her lip nervously.

Eric squeezed her hand gently and smiled reassuringly. "Possibly. I'll send a note to Noah and see what he says."

Claire nodded, but he could tell she wasn't sure about any of this. Her world had been rocked, and now she needed stability. He hoped he could give it to her.

CHAPTER TWENTY-SEVEN

They spent the next few days making love, which Claire really liked, taking walks which was a nice way to get to know the town, and learning each other's likes and dislikes. She found out that Eric hated peas the hard way. Luckily, they laughed it off, and he fixed himself a grilled cheese sandwich while she ate her pea and chicken casserole.

With her family, there'd always been an edge in every interaction. With Eric, that hardness was gone. She felt like she could be herself, and it was a relief.

When the weekend ended, Eric had to return to work, leaving Claire alone. She needed to find a job. It wasn't just the money. She didn't want to spend all day alone. She didn't know what type of job she should look for. Maybe she just needed to get out of the house.

Would April be working at Grinders today? She decided she needed to find out. Maybe April wouldn't be there, but it would be nice to see her again. She knew April was heading out in a few months, but the woman seemed cool and was around her age.

Claire took one last look around Eric's cozy little house, thinking she really liked living in Fallport with Eric.

She opened the door to Grinders and was hit by a wall of laughter. She found the source. A group of women were crowded around a table, with coffee and muffins in front of them.

"Hey, it's Claire," April called out as she stepped inside.

The women all turned to stare at her, and she smiled, lifting her hand as a wave of shyness hit. For a moment, she worried they would shun her. She'd experienced that in more than one place they'd moved. Heck, in Baltimore, she hadn't really made any friends, but that was mainly because she'd been working all the time, and all of her friends from high school had left the city.

"Claire, it's nice to meet you. I think you've met my man. I'm Lilly, and this is Elsie. Bristol is to my left, and Caryn is across from me."

There was no way she would keep up with their names. She felt a little overwhelmed. "I don't really know anyone here but Eric. How do I know your man?" Claire asked.

"He was on the rescue mission. You may not

remember him. Maybe you didn't actually meet him. I'm not sure how that played out."

Claire nodded, feeling a little more relaxed. "I'm so thankful they were out there. I would have died. Eric saved me."

The women all nodded. April pulled over another chair. "Take a seat. I'll fix you a coffee. What would you like?"

"I like vanilla lattes," Claire said.

"Coming right up." April moved behind the bar.

"We have extra muffins," Lilly said.

"It's crazy how lost you can get in the forest," one of the women said. She was fit, muscular, more like an athlete than a regular person. "I'm Caryn, by the way. I know it's hard to keep up with names."

Claire took a bite of muffin and then nodded. "There's no way I'll remember all of your names."

They all laughed. "After a while, you'll know us all. I'm Elsie. I'm with Zeke."

Claire swallowed another bite of the muffin before speaking. "He's from the bar, right? I remember meeting him."

Elsie nodded. "Yeah, he owns the bar."

"I like that place, and he's nice. He introduced me to Drew."

"That's my man," Caryn said.

Claire turned to her and flashed a smile. "Drew might just save my hide. I probably shouldn't talk about it, but everything is messed up."

Lilly reached out and put her hand on Claire's shoulder. "We're here for you if you need us."

"They mean that," April said. "We all do. They saved me last year when I was stalked. They are good people. Oh, and Caryn is also on the search and rescue team."

Claire turned to her and blinked. "Were you there that night I was abducted?"

Caryn shook her head. "No, we had some other stuff to do. But that's why it's a team. We all work together, kind of like this town. I know it may seem overwhelming, but this is a good place."

Claire's eyes started to burn. She didn't want to cry, but she just might. "Thank you, all. It means a lot having nice people around me. I have a meeting with the FBI agent tomorrow, so hopefully, it will get better."

"We meet here on Monday mornings before some of us head to work," Lilly said.

"Oh, crap, work," Caryn said. "I'm running late. I'll see you all later."

"Oh, I have a meeting," Elsie said as she stood. She hugged Claire before taking off.

Bristol stood, too. "I have a call in a few. It was nice meeting you."

"It was great meeting all of you. I'll remember about Monday morning here."

"Good, we'd love to see you again," Bristol said before she waved and walked out.

Claire finished her muffin and picked up her coffee. She followed Lilly outside.

"Thank you for letting me join you this morning."

"Of course. I love this place. I think you will, too. Give it some time, and everything will work out."

Lilly gave her a quick hug before turning around. Claire walked across the street, thinking about the town and where she should apply for a job, when someone stepped onto the path in front of her. She didn't recognize the man for a second, then she realized it was Blaine, her brother. Mike stepped onto the path behind him.

"You're gonna pay," Blaine said.

"You brought the feds down on us. Dad's in jail right now, you bitch."

Fear hit hard, and she froze for a second, trying to figure out what she could do. April was alone at Grinders, and most other businesses were closed. She didn't know which way the police station was. All she knew was she had to get away from her brothers.

She tossed her half-consumed coffee on the grass and took off, dashing across the square. She ran past the post office and almost ran into someone. Seconds later, she realized it was Otto.

Fear closed her throat, and it kept her from screaming. She was maybe twenty feet in front of her brothers, but they would catch up. She needed a clear escape.

Blaine called out her name as he chased after her. She glanced back, not seeing Mike. Where was he? She didn't have time to look around. They would kill her. No question, they'd come here to do something bad.

"We'll make you regret going to the feds!" Blaine screamed as she rounded the corner and ran past the barbershop toward some houses. Only then did she remember the police station wasn't this way.

Claire ran faster, pushing herself past her limits as she tried to escape them. Her heart pounded, and sweat broke out on her brow as she darted down streets she'd never seen.

She thought she might have escaped when suddenly a car pulled out, and she had to stop or run into it. She moved to go around the car when the door opened, and Mike jumped out. Shock coursed through her, and she froze.

Then Blaine was there, shoving her into the open trunk. If they closed the lid, she would die. With all her strength, she fought them, but then Blaine punched her, knocking her back.

The trunk lid closed, and darkness prevailed. Eric would have no idea where she'd gone. He'd just think she left. Tears streamed down her cheeks. The noise of the car drowned out her cries for help. She was caught, and there wasn't anything she could do.

CHAPTER TWENTY-EIGHT

Eric hammered in the nail, satisfied with his work. Desmond came over, admiring what he'd done.

"Wow, that's amazing. I'm glad you're feeling better."

"Same, but I miss spending time with Claire," Eric said.

"She's the one you got shot for. It's amazing that you both made it out. I'd heard those were some real bad guys."

"Yeah. I guess that guy who shot me is out of the hospital and in jail."

Desmond chuckled. "Yeah, I heard he was whining all the way to the hospital. I mean, he did break both legs and an arm, but he was willing to kill you both. I don't really feel sorry for him."

"Thanks for letting me come back to work this week. I miss doing stuff like this."

Desmond nodded. "We probably won't have another house like this for a while."

Eric glanced around. "It's crazy this guy wants this huge of a house here. But whatever. It's his money."

"Yeah, crazy." Desmond glanced around. "You know, I could give him a portfolio of your furniture if you like."

Eric put his hands on his hips and turned to Desmond. "You'd do that for me? That's awesome. A house like this, I could probably live for a year off the commissions."

Desmond threw back his head, laughter spilling out. "You know it. And the guy is willing to spend his money, so go for it."

Eric got back to work and was about to measure for some wood paneling when his phone rang. It was Otto. He answered, wondering what the man wanted. "Hello, it's Eric."

"They got her."

"What?"

"I ran after them, but I was slow. I called Hill and the cops are trying to find her, but she's gone."

Panic raced through Eric. Otto was talking about Claire. There's no one else this man would call him about. "Do you have any idea which way they went?"

"No. I couldn't keep up. She runs too fast. They're in a green sedan. I gave the cops the description, but they could be anywhere."

"Shit." Eric spun around, looking for Desmond. The

man must have realized something had gone wrong and moved closer. He ended the call with Otto, thanking him for calling.

"What's wrong?"

"Someone abducted Claire."

"Again?" Desmond asked.

Eric's phone rang, and he saw it was Lilly. He thought about shoving it to voicemail, but it could be Ethan.

"Yeah," Eric said.

"I saw it happen," Lilly said, her voice raised over the car noise filtering in.

"What did you see?" Eric asked.

"I was following but lost them when they turned onto Green Mountain Run Road."

"Shit, that's where I am," Eric said.

"Be careful. The cops know which way they went. They should be headed that way now."

Eric ended the call and met Desmond's gaze. "They're headed up this road, Green Mountain Run."

"Shit," Desmond looked around. "Maybe some of the guys have guns in their trucks. I'm calling everyone to stop." Desmond called out, yelling for everyone to meet outside the house.

This place was almost at the end of the road, with only parking for a trailhead about five hundred yards down. Eric didn't know if he trusted these men to not shoot Claire, but they had little choice. He didn't know who had taken Claire hostage, but he needed to save her.

"Eric's woman was taken hostage," Desmond began.

"Again?" a few of the guys said.

It was unbelievable that Claire had been abducted again. Eric knew that. But there were evil people around her who didn't mind taking advantage of her. It could be the same group as last time or one of her family members. He didn't care who it was. He just knew he had to save her.

"We need to help if we can," Desmond said.

"The cops are headed this way, so help is coming."

"I'm gonna get my gun," one of the guys said.

"Damn straight," another man said.

"Just be careful," Eric called out after them. "Don't shoot Claire and don't let the cops shoot you."

Panic wove through Eric. Like most men in the area, he had a shotgun in his truck. It was just how life operated here. Sometimes on worksites, they found venomous snakes, and it was safer to shoot them than let them wander off and eventually bite one of the workers.

Eric grabbed his shotgun and moved to the road, unsure what good he could do. Two guys hopped in their truck and took off, driving toward the parking spot for the trailhead. His heart was in his throat, and his brain buzzed. Maybe this was the wrong thing to do. They shouldn't be out here with guns, but how else could he help Claire?

The sound of tires crunching on gravel filtered through the trees. The road was winding, and it would be a while before they could see the car. He prayed the jerks didn't stop before they made the last curve to the house. If Claire was this close and he didn't save her, he would forever regret everything.

Maybe he should get in his truck and go find them. But then he could cause a wreck and injure Claire. Shit, he had no good options.

Anticipation built, and he was about to race toward his truck when a green sedan came into view. He didn't know what to do. The car was moving too fast and fishtailed as it finished the curve. Fear blasted through him. He needed them to stop, but if he jumped out into the road, the driver could just run into him.

Desmond moved fast, stepping into the road and raising his gun. Eric wanted to tell him to move, but there wasn't time. The driver, who looked surprisingly like Claire's brother, slammed on the brakes, and the car spun around.

Eric feared they would take off the other way, but like most roads in this area, the sides of the roads weren't meant for driving on, and the back end of the car went over too far, dropping the tire into a deep ditch. The driver tried to gun it, but the car wasn't going anywhere.

He wouldn't hesitate. Eric moved fast, running toward the car. The passenger door opened, and the guy stepped out, raising a pistol. Desmond was already set up and fired his shotgun. Desmond wasn't too close and must not have had buckshot loaded because the guy screamed and dropped his gun but wasn't knocked on his ass.

The other man got out and ran toward the back of the car, but he couldn't get there. He ran around, which was a mistake because Eric blocked his way. The next move was a no-brainer. Eric slammed the butt of his gun into the guy's head, knocking him down.

The sound of sirens split the air, and Eric knew salvation was close. Desmond and the other men took over, securing the two guys Eric thought were Claire's brothers.

"Where is she?" Eric screamed.

Her brothers flinched, and Eric wanted to cause them pain. Anger swirled so close to his fear that he thought he might lose it. The haze of blood rushing through his veins made it hard to hear anything, but he finally heard pounding over the sirens and his anger.

Eric turned and stared at the back of the car where the noise came from. She was in the trunk and making a racket. That meant she wasn't dead.

Relief almost dropped him to his knees. He moved to the trunk and realized he couldn't open it without keys. He glanced at the car's back seat and saw a plastic tab that probably made the seats fold down. He opened the back door and lifted the tab, freeing three-quarters of the back seat so it folded down.

He could see Claire in the dim light streaming in,

and he saw her head whip around. Their gazes met, and then she moved, crawling through the opening and into his arms.

Adrenalin pumping through his system made him shake as he pulled her close. She was safe. Maybe a little bruised, but she was in his arms and free from kidnappers once again.

"Is that your brothers?" he asked once he could speak.

"Yes," she choked out over her sobs.

He pulled her closer, glad he had found her. So much could have gone wrong. Her brothers could have driven a different way. They could have killed her before they made it this far. She could have been lost to him forever.

It took about an hour for the police to sort through everything. By then, Eric was able to drive. He met Claire at the doctor's office, glad to see that she was okay. She only needed a small bandage where she'd been cut and some over-the-counter pain medicine for the bruises.

"You saved me again." Claire flashed him a wobbly smile.

He pulled her into a hug, never wanting to let go. "Lilly called. That's the only reason we knew you were coming up that road."

Her eyes went round. "It's so weird my brothers drove up here."

He nodded, relief flooding his body. "Yeah, they

must have panicked when they realized people had seen them take you."

"Do you think people saw?"

"Otto called me and the cops."

She pulled back, her eyes wide. "So Otto saved me, too."

He nodded. "The police chief said there were multiple people who called it in. This town watches out for people."

Claire blew out a breath. "I think my brothers will be locked up for a long time."

"I think so. They kidnapped you and had plans to kill you. The chief found texts on their phones."

"God, to think my family was so evil."

"I'm sorry. But I want you to know I'm here for you." Eric held her gaze, the love plainly evident in his eyes. "I love you. Like I said before, I was falling for you, and it's true. We may not have known each other long, but my love is real."

"I love you, too."

He clung to her, never wanting to let her go. They had love, which he knew Claire would need to lean on. She'd lost her family, but since they were willing to frame her and then kill her, it really wasn't that huge of a loss. He just hoped she saw it.

CHAPTER TWENTY-NINE

Claire was thankful she had Eric. The man was amazing and showed her how much she was loved every day. They were outside one of his friend's house, grilling hamburgers and hot dogs. April was there, along with Mac.

Brock, the guy who owned the house, came over. "Hey, how are you two doing?"

"Good," Eric said.

She nodded. "Real good."

"Awesome. I'm glad you both came," Brock said.

Ethan and Lilly lifted their glasses. "We feel the same. We're glad you're safe."

Drew moved closer. "I heard that the FBI is moving forward with their case."

Claire nodded. "They are. Sadly, I lost my family. I just can't believe they were willing to do everything they did. It feels terrible."

"Well, you know you're a part of our family now, right?" Lilly said.

She nodded as Bristol came over and hugged her. "That's not just lip service. We all want you to have a good life. You are family."

"Hear, hear," Brock said. "To family!"

Everyone joined in, lifting their glass to his toast. It was odd. She felt like these people were more like family to her than her own parents and brothers had been. Since the cops had arrested her brothers, the people of Fallport had rallied around her. She had a job now at the local school answering phones. That allowed her to play with a folk band at Zeke's bar once a week. People wished her well and bought her coffee. They truly wanted to help her adjust to living in Fallport.

But most of all, she'd found a real family with Eric. They were planning on getting married next Christmas. He said he wanted to start a new tradition with her of celebrating everything good. And Christmas was the holiday they chose to tie the knot on. She was thrilled and couldn't imagine a better time of the year for such a great celebration.

She had no idea how much everything would change when she'd planned her trip to Fallport with her family. This town had been central to her future, and the man beside her was now central to her life.

She glanced up, meeting Eric's gaze. "Hey, love. You good?"

She snuggled up close, kissing his cheek. "So good, love. So good." And she was. Everything with Eric was good.

The End

Saving Lorelei

Rescuing Amy

Saving Sloan

Seeking Justice

Justice for Amber

Searching for Keeley

Justice for Oswin

Safety for Eve

Dark Eagle Series

Survive The Fall

Live Past The Edge

Hold on Through the Pain

Endure the Darkness

Storm Corp Series

Determined

Standalone Romance

Acting The Part

All Business

Just One Taste

Unseen Cruelty

ABOUT THE AUTHOR

Julia Bright is the author of the contemporary military romance Dark Eagle series and is an Operation Alpha Author. Julia lives in the south where "bless your heart" is an insult and "shut up" shows love. Julia has been reading since they could open a book and has taken the passion for words and combined it with the love of travel to create stories full of passion and excitement. If you love a good book with a fantastic happily ever after, you'll enjoy a Julia Bright novel. For a dash of paranormal romance and urban fantasy, pick up a book from Julia's USA Today Bestselling JS Bright per name

facebook.com/AuthorJuliaBright

amazon.com/Julia-Bright/e

bookbub.com/authors/julia-bright

There are many more books in this fan fiction world than listed here, for an up-to-date list go to www.AcesPress.com

You can also visit our Amazon page at:
http://www.amazon.com/author/operationalpha

Special Forces: Operation Alpha World
Christie Adams: Charity's Heart
Linzi Baxter: Dangerous Rescue
Misha Blake: Flash
Anna Blakely: Rescuing Gracelynn
Julia Bright: Saving Lorelei
Cara Carnes: Protecting Mari
Kendra Mei Chailyn: Beast
Melissa Kay Clarke: Rescuing Annabeth
Samantha A. Cole: Handling Haven
Lorelei Confer: Protecting Sara
KaLyn Cooper: Spring Unveiled
Janie Crouch: Storm
Jordan Dane: Redemption for Avery
Tarina Deaton: Found in the Lost
Riley Edwards: Protecting Olivia
Dorothy Ewels: Knight's Queen
Lila Ferrari: Protecting Joy
Nicole Flockton: Protecting Maria
Hope Ford: Rescuing Karina
Amy Gamet: Guarded by the SEAL

Desiree Holt: Protecting Maddie
Jesse Jacobson: Protecting Honor
Rayne Lewis: Justice for Mary
Ireland Lorelei: The Detective
Kristin Lynn: Worth the Risk
Callie Love & Ann Omasta: Hawaii Hottie
JM Madden: Rescuing Olivia
A.M. Mahler: Griffin
Ellie Masters: Sybil's Protector
Trish McCallan: Hero Under Fire
Rachel McNeely: The SEAL's Surprise Baby
KD Michaels: Saving Laura
Olivia Michaels: Protecting Harper
Annie Miller: Securing Willow
Keira Montclair: Wolf and the Wild Scots
MJ Nightingale: Protecting Beauty
Melinda Owens: Betraying Katie
Victoria Paige: Reclaiming Izabel
Danielle Pays: Defending Sarina
Lainey Reese: Protecting New York
KeKe Renée: Protecting Bria
TL Reeve and Michele Ryan: Extracting Mateo
Deanna L. Rowley: Saving Veronica
Angela Rush: Charlotte
Rose Smith: Saving Satin
Tyler Anne Snell: Cowboy Heat
Lynne St. James: SEAL's Spitfire
E.M. Shue: Discovering Tyler
Bella Stone: Rexar

Jen Talty: Burning Desire
Reina Torres, Rescuing Hi'ilani
LJ Vickery: Circus Comes to Town
R. C. Wynne: Shadows Renewed

Delta Team Three Series
Lori Ryan: Nori's Delta
Becca Jameson: Destiny's Delta
Lynne St James, Gwen's Delta
Elle James: Ivy's Delta
Riley Edwards: Hope's Delta

Police and Fire: Operation Alpha World
Freya Barker: Burning for Autumn
B.P. Beth: Scott
Jane Blythe: Salvaging Marigold
Julia Bright, Justice for Amber
Hadley Finn: Exton
Emily Gray: Shelter for Allegra
Deanndra Hall: Shelter for Sharla
Jenna Harte: Dead But Not Forgotten
India Kells: Shadow Killer
Amber Kuhlman: Protecting Paisley
Reina Torres: Justice for Sloane
Aubree Valentine, Justice for Danielle
Maddie Wade: Finding English

Tarpley VFD Series
Silver James, Fighting for Elena

Deanndra Hall, Fighting for Carly
Haven Rose, Fighting for Calliope
MJ Nightingale, Fighting for Jemma
TL Reeve, Fighting for Brittney
Nicole Flockton, Fighting for Nadia

As you know, this book included at least one character from Susan Stoker's books. To check out more, see below.

SEAL Team Hawaii Series
Finding Elodie
Finding Lexie
Finding Kenna
Finding Monica
Finding Carly
Finding Ashlyn
Finding Jodelle (July 2023)

Eagle Point Search & Rescue
Searching for Lilly
Searching for Elsie
Searching for Bristol
Searching for Caryn
Searching for Finley (Sept 2023)
Searching for Heather (Jan 2024)
Searching for Khloe (TBA)

The Refuge Series
Deserving Alaska
Deserving Henley
Deserving Reese
Deserving Cora (Nov 2023)
Deserving Lara (Feb 2024)
Deserving Maisy (TBA)

Deserving Ryleigh (TBA)

Delta Team Two Series

Shielding Gillian
Shielding Kinley
Shielding Aspen
Shielding Jayme (novella)
Shielding Riley
Shielding Devyn
Shielding Ember
Shielding Sierra

SEAL of Protection: Legacy Series

Securing Caite (FREE!)
Securing Brenae (novella)
Securing Sidney
Securing Piper
Securing Zoey
Securing Avery
Securing Kalee
Securing Jane

Delta Force Heroes Series

Rescuing Rayne (FREE!)
Rescuing Aimee (novella)
Rescuing Emily
Rescuing Harley
Marrying Emily (novella)
Rescuing Kassie

Rescuing Bryn

Rescuing Casey

Rescuing Sadie (novella)

Rescuing Wendy

Rescuing Mary

Rescuing Macie (novella)

Rescuing Annie

Badge of Honor: Texas Heroes Series

Justice for Mackenzie (FREE!)

Justice for Mickie

Justice for Corrie

Justice for Laine (novella)

Shelter for Elizabeth

Justice for Boone

Shelter for Adeline

Shelter for Sophie

Justice for Erin

Justice for Milena

Shelter for Blythe

Justice for Hope

Shelter for Quinn

Shelter for Koren

Shelter for Penelope

SEAL of Protection Series

Protecting Caroline (FREE!)

Protecting Alabama

Protecting Fiona

Marrying Caroline (novella)
Protecting Summer
Protecting Cheyenne
Protecting Jessyka
Protecting Julie (novella)
Protecting Melody
Protecting the Future
Protecting Kiera (novella)
Protecting Alabama's Kids (novella)
Protecting Dakota

New York Times, *USA Today* and *Wall Street Journal* Bestselling Author Susan Stoker has a heart as big as the state of Tennessee where she lives, but this all American girl has also spent the last fourteen years living in Missouri, California, Colorado, Indiana, and Texas. She's married to a retired Army man who now gets to follow *her* around the country.

www.stokeraces.com
www.AcesPress.com
susan@stokeraces.com

Made in the USA
Coppell, TX
10 June 2023

17913883R00136